P9-AEV-876

The Art of Christian Meditation

David Ray

A Guide to
Increase Your Personal
Awareness
of God

TYNDALE HOUSE PUBLISHERS, INC.
Wheaton, Illinois

Key to Bible versions:
RSV–Revised Standard Version
TEV–Today's English Version, American Bible Society
NEB–New English Bible, Oxford University Press, Cambridge University Press
TLB–The Living Bible, Tyndale House Publishers

The Art of Christian Meditation. Library of Congress Catalog Card Number 77-080736. ISBN 0-8423-0087-2, paper. Copyright © 1977, by Tyndale House Publishers, Inc., Wheaton, Illinois. All rights reserved. Second printing, January 1978. Printed in the United States of America.

For information write: Christian Meditation Association, Incorporated, 1100 West Capitol Street, Jackson, Mississippi 39203.

Contents

When in the Night I Meditate

When in the night I meditate
On mercies multiplied,
My grateful heart inspires my tongue
To bless the Lord, my Guide.

My inmost being thrills with joy
And gladness fills my breast;
Because on Him my trust is stayed,
My flesh in hope shall rest.

The path of life Thou showest me;
Of joy a boundless store
Is ever found at Thy right hand,
And pleasures evermore.

From *The Hymnbook*
C. M. Maitland
George N. Allen

Introduction

What has happened to our awareness of the meditative Jesus, who found his strength in quietness and confidence, who often removed himself from the crowds to ponder and pray, and who personally experienced the power of the awareness of God? We have dismissed to the sidelines this view of our Lord, and thus have overlooked the dynamic role of meditation in our own lives. Sucked in by a modern, sophisticated, and industrialized civilization with an overemphasis on "doing" and a dwarfed emphasis on "being," we have left the quiet, powerful, and healthy practice of meditation to gurus, mystics, and oriental religions.

I for one looked with suspicion on any movement that advocated such a practice as meditation. "They're out of contact with reality," I thought. "Nonsense! Give me action and work, lots of work! Let somebody else waste time staring at the end of his nose!"

Then something began to happen as I read Psalm 46:10 and allowed it to soak into my thoughts.

Be still, and know that I am God.

I had read the verse hundreds of times, but this time the words "still," "know," and "God," in that sequence began to lunge at me. Questions popped up like, "How well do I know God?" "How far have I come since I professed faith in Jesus Christ?" "Could there be something more real and concrete to my experience?" "How aware am I, at this moment, of God's presence?"

The answer from my innermost heart revealed that life can be much better. Then the word "still" became the hub of my thinking. I realized that to know God, I needed to be still in a creative way, to cease from activity at times during the day, and to focus my uninterrupted attention on God.

Well, the outgrowth of this silent revolution is what I call "The Art of Christian Meditation." This meditation involves form, significant content, and glorious results.

Amazingly, my activity level has not shrunk one iota. Rather, it has been raised. My consciousness of being a person in the world has not shriveled a tidbit, and I have not suffered the "other-world, out-of-touch" syndrome. Instead, I have become more conscious of the world in which God has placed me. Through Christian meditation, I have become more aware that I am a real person in a real world with a genuine religious faith.

Furthermore, through Christian meditation I have been able to fasten myself to something real, definite, and visible each day. The practice of meditating has increased my personal awareness of the presence of God.

I am finding that other believers also feel a need for Christian meditation. This need eventually led me to develop the Christian Meditation Seminars. Since I am unable to go everywhere for seminars, I have been asked to share the message of Christian meditation with as many people as possible. What better way than through a book?

Most sincerely,
David Ray

I Came to It
the Hard Way

I had just started those inquisitive, perilous, challenging teen years. Perry Kenner, a businessman in my hometown of Abilene, Texas, asked me to attend the seventh grade class he taught in Sunday school. Perry persistently phoned me each week. "How are you doing, David? I've been thinking about you. I'd like to see you in class on Sunday." To insure my presence, he volunteered to drop by on the way so that I could ride with him.

It was through his dedication that I began to honestly believe there is a personal God who might care about *me*. It wasn't that I had ever deliberately disbelieved. Rather, I had never really thought about how God related to my life in a personal way.

My interest gradually perked up. And, one by one, little reservations subsided. Before the year ended, this lanky, freckle-faced thirteen-year-old slipped on his knees in the quietness of the church. I offered myself, just as I was and as completely as I knew how, to Jesus Christ. The occasion was serious, but without fanfare and hullabaloo.

Frankly, my level of understanding of the church, creeds, and church fathers was very shallow. In fact, it was almost nonexistent. Furthermore, I was embarrassingly short on knowledge of the Bible. Actually, there was only one point in my favor. In my heart of hearts, I sensed that God truly loved me; that he would receive me as I was; and that I needed him. I saw myself as a person for whom God cared in spite of my shortcomings.

I believe that God accepted me into his redeemed family and that his acceptance launched the "we" relationship (God and me) of partnership. In retrospect, I think of that conversion in terms of God finding me in a personal way. God was the hunter and I was the hunted: God sought me out, took unerring aim, fired, and hit the bull's-eye.

But my commitment to God did not solve my difficulties

9

forevermore. For one thing, *I have remained a human being.* To my surprise, my faith incurred a paradox. It has been twenty-seven years since I began personally on the journey of God's grace; yet the longer I live, the more I sense a need for God.

As my friend Lane Adams asks in his book of the same title, *How Come It's Taking Me So Long to Get Better?* I'm reminded of a comment made by one of my parishioners. A couple was about to be married. As some of us waited for the organist to sound the processional, a friend wished the groom a happy marriage. The best man, a member of my congregation, said, "Every marriage is happy. It's the living together afterward which gets sticky!"

I find that I still have to live with myself, and with those three levels of consciousness—waking, sleeping, and dreaming—which need to increasingly come under the redeeming power of God's presence.

Besides, I have to face wife, children, parents, brothers, sister, in-laws, peers, events (expected and unexpected), pressures, problems, the past, the future, and, in general, the demands of everyday living.

I found that the rational and emotional sides of my personality were not instantly harmonized. Anxiety was not permanently banned in one initial swoop of faith and God's love.

In my experience as a minister, I have found that I am not alone. Often sincere believers in need of peace of mind, love, joy, patience, kindness, humility, and self-control (to mention only a few qualities) have sought help from me. Added to their distress has been a layer of guilt because they thought they were one of a kind. "After all, *Christians* don't have such weaknesses." They had assumed that anyone with a viable faith in Jesus Christ surely had to be 100 percent adjusted to God, self, others, and things; they had concluded that they must be stepchildren of God rather than the real McCoy.

I recall my conversation with a young housewife. Her husband asked that I see her because he felt she might be on the verge of emotional collapse. "Sometimes," she said, "I feel like there are two 'mes' inside. There's one wanting to become a more genuine, growing Christian. I take my new commitment to God and the church seriously. But there is the 'me' pulling toward that old way of life which is wrong."

She was like the man who called for an appointment. During our talk he said, "I would know myself better if there were not so many of me."

As sincere as the woman was, she thought that total change would come about overnight.

The apostle Paul referred to this dilemma when he wrote:

> So I find it to be a law that when I want to do right, evil lies close at hand. For I delight in the law of God, in my inmost self, but I see in my members another law at war with the law of my mind... (Rom. 7:21-23, RSV).

Of course, the unmitigated truth is that people of Christ are still persons in a world where the rain does not always distinguish between the just and the unjust. At times, both get wet!

As a professing Christian, I have had to squarely face that fact. Furthermore, I have been forced by my own human nature and the requirements of living in a rapidly changing, fast-moving, technological age to admit that I need a progressive orientation to and identification with the God I acknowledge.

With these realities in mind a few years ago, I began to focus my need into three basic areas.

REINFORCEMENT

One of my needs has been for reinforcement of the spirit I experienced when I confessed my faith.

As Paul wrote, "If any one is in Christ, he is a new creation; the old has passed away, behold, the new has come" (2 Cor. 5:17, RSV). As the Psalmist puts it, we are "wonderfully made" (139:14).

At the time I accepted Christ I had a new peace of mind, a simply marvelous sense of love, and an outlook on life that filled it with meaning and direction. I had immense joy in living and an honest pleasure in being alive. A new spirit ushered me into a completely fresh and wonderful realization of myself as one made in the image of God. I had a genuine desire and eager willingness to follow the guidelines of my new faith as I understood them. I had the confidence of a reliable power enabling me to cope with the demands of life and to convert setbacks into successes. (I must admit that those demands have accelerated over the years.) This new platform for thought, activity, and aspirations brought a vitality to each day that amazed me and, I suspect, my parents, two brothers, a sister, teachers, and teen-age friends.

My faith seemed as up-to-date as the morning sun.

Now, should anyone lose these advantages as he "settles" in his faith? Are they like old clothes to be discarded after a year or two of wear? Certainly not! Rather, such characteristics are meant to continue and increase. Their foundations are to be strengthened.

However, that does not happen without daily application.

Such application causes reinforcement of the positive aspects of life which God wants me to enjoy (which I really *want* to enjoy) and the positive benefits which I want to obtain.

For me, reinforcement of the new self on a regular schedule has become essential to my advancement and happiness in the Christian life.

REPROGRAMMING

The unconscious side of personality is like a computer which stores up data that is supplied to it by the conscious mind through parents, peers, events, and other influences. Think of it as a filing cabinet of thoughts and experiences you have had. I am told that nothing we see or hear is ever lost. It is put into the unconscious self.

In researching the unconscious mind, some scientists have inserted an instrument into the brain to provide stimulus so that patients have instantly relived events in their past. One woman vividly described the music she heard at a symphony concert which she had attended years earlier. The concert was the one and only time she had ever been exposed to the music. Someone else lived an event in childhood which he had not consciously thought of since it happened.

They were not acting on memory. They were really living, acting, and again experiencing those events. Having once been exposed to the events, they had seemed to forget, but the experiences were not erased. They had passed into the unconscious mind.

Besides the unconscious mind, there are certain actions or habits which have been grooved into our systems of thought and activity. A new beginning will get a person going in another direction, but the beginning is exactly what the word implies—a start. To develop a new and lasting system of thought and activity, I realized that I needed to program my spiritual self daily. Gradually my life began to be retracked. I got on a consistent and regular schedule, retreating from the less desirable self—the part of me bent on wrongful attitudes, actions, and responses—and the inevitable defeat those responses bring.

RELEASE

My third need has been to experience release and discover my full potential as a child of God. After some time into my relationship with God, I discovered that he always holds before me the challenge to keep growing up. In that way, a new adventure always lies a step ahead. There is always a new mountain to climb, go around, tunnel under, or shovel through. There is a new frontier to explore and a fresh, added dimension of life within reach.

These achievements were attainable, but not from the platform of a stale, dried-up, static religious experience. Rather, they came when I pioneered in faith, daring to undergo release of potential, day by day, in God.

As a result, I have found a new freedom, a day at a time, from stress and anxiety. I have a new respect for all of God's creation.

I have experienced cleansing and renewal in God's forgiveness, character and personality improvement, a higher energy level, a deeper relaxation, a clarity of thought and perception, a sharper performance, and an emotional and social stability. Yet, I must admit that, as the TV commercial says, "I've only just begun."

Then, over a period of years, the question became: What guidelines would best serve me in developing reinforcement, reprogramming, and release? I jotted down a list of ideas which became awkwardly long. After careful evaluation, I decided on characteristics which any course of action for me must include.

1. SIMPLICITY

It had to be uncomplicated, and remain uncomplicated, yet redeeming.

2. TOTALITY

The course of action had to pertain to me as a human being and deal with me as a total person—body, mind, and spirit.

3. APPLICABILITY

It had to be a process I could readily absorb and apply so that it would affect me where I live.

4. ENJOYABILITY

It had to be interesting so that my attention could be maintained.

5. MEASURABILITY

The course of action had to be one by which I could effect positive change, with measurable results.

6. RESPONSIBILITY

The process had to be one for which I, and I alone, was responsible before God. I believe that the freedom to be responsible is one of the great remaining freedoms of the individual.

ANSWER

Considering the guidelines I had set up in trying to determine my course of action, I found that Christian meditation provided the ideal answer.

What Is Christian Meditation? 2

One of my favorite cartoons is "Peanuts." In one scene, the gang is playing softball with Lucy as shortstop and Charlie Brown behind the plate. A lazy pop-up is hit to Lucy. She can easily catch it, but she stands there as the ball drops about a foot in front of her. Charlie Brown runs out screaming, "Why didn't you catch the ball?" Lucy answers, "I was meditating."

The word "meditate" means to "think upon." The Psalmist writes, "When I *think* of thee upon my bed, and meditate on thee in the watches of the night" (Psa. 63:6, RSV). Quakers in the old days called it "centering down."

Our root word for "meditation" is of Greek origin and means "to measure out." "Medical" is derived from the same root word and it implies that there is a healing value to meditation. In other words, meditation works on your spiritual self in a creative way, and the effects are seen in your physical self.

Similar to dieting, meditation is something which you must do in order to achieve the benefits it offers. It's hard, but you must begin to work at it. I am reminded of the story told by Bishop Fulton J. Sheen about a fat woman who went to the gymnasium. She asked the instructor what she must do to lose weight. The instructor said that she must chin herself fifty times a day, and the woman asked, "Which chin?"

Christian meditation is something you must do because you *can* do it. It is faith plus works. Christian meditation is a case of keeping your mind on God and your hands on the plow. As the apostle Paul wrote, "... I keep *working* toward that day when I will finally be all that Christ saved me for and wants me to be" (Phil. 3:12, TLB).

In meditation you concern yourself with what you can do. Your conscious acts of meditation involve prompting and suggestion. In turn, they pry into your unconscious mind and bring a new and penetrating relaxation. Thus Christian medita-

16

tion may be a healthy spiritual discipline—one that bears fruit.

Christian meditation, purely and simply, means to center your thoughts on God by a deliberate practice. Dr. Charlie Shedd in his book *Getting Through to the Wonderful You* calls it "getting in touch with the divine Presence." As recorded in Luke 17:21, Jesus spoke of his disciples as having the kingdom of God *within* them. As a believer, Christ lives in you. He is the tremendous source of divine, creative intelligence working in you. You have the spirit of Christ!

CONSCIOUS THOUGHT

Even though you have within you the spirit of Jesus Christ, you have a profound need which continues unabated. This need is to focus your conscious thought on God every day. One shot of faith at any one specific time does not satisfy that need for all the days thereafter. By centering your conscious thought on God *a day at a time,* you increase in your awareness of God. More than a process of emptying the mind, it is a filling of the mind. Also it is more than getting your thoughts off something, although, to be sure, you accomplish exactly that by getting your thoughts *on* something—Jesus Christ.

SIGNIFICANT CONTENT

Christian meditation is meditation with significant content, because it is rooted in a knowledge of God himself. Dr. C. J. Jung, a widely acclaimed psychologist, alludes to the basic difference between Christian meditation and other forms in his book, *Psychology and Religion: East and West.* "Between the Christian and Buddhist [method of meditation] there is a subtle but enormous difference. The Christian during contemplation would never say 'I am Christ,' but will confess with Paul: 'Not I, but Christ liveth in me' [Gal. 2:20]. [The Buddhist form], however, says, 'Thou wilt know that thou art the Buddha' … The Christian attains his end in Christ."

PURPOSE

The purpose of Christian meditation is not withdrawal from the society in which you live or from all of the stress, problems, change, time, and anxiety you face. Instead, through Christian meditation, you are drawn to God and you grow in an awareness of his presence on the very level where you live, work, and play. The essential purpose of Christian meditation is to increase your personal awareness of God.

Consequently, you are drawn upward, step-by-step, into a greater circle of God's wholeness by which you are enabled to fully live in today's world. In turn, you are drawn out into your world as a person to act within society. Through meditation you get in rhythm with God's forces at work in the universe.

TOTAL PERSON

A close evaluation of the Gospels has shown me that Jesus dealt with the complete man through forgiveness of sins, healing of mind and body, healing of disposition, habits, morals, memories, relationships, ambitions, realities, the past, and the present.

Paul wrote clearly on this matter.

> ... The body is [meant] for the Lord, and the Lord for the body. Do you not know that your bodies are members of Christ? Do you not know that your body is a temple of the Holy Spirit within you...? (1 Cor. 6:13, 15, 19, RSV).

I believe that what the apostle wrote about the church in 1 Corinthians, chapter 12, can also be applied here:

> For the body does not consist of one member but of many [hands, eyes, ears, noses, feet, etc.] ... If one member suffers, all suffer together (vv. 14, 26, RSV).

When the finger hurts, in a sense, the soul hurts. (Have you seen anyone laugh when he slammed a door shut on his finger?) When the spirit experiences a feeling of joy, the body joins in the celebration. (The body perks up.) When the mind droops with pessimism, orderly and wholesome functions of the body are interrupted. (For example, loss of weight when there is prolonged depression.)

Christian meditation involves the *total* person—body, mind, spirit. Christian meditation does not fragment and compartmentalize you. Instead, each aspect of your person is enabled to complement, enhance, and contribute to the others. Taking each part of you into consideration, Christian meditation blesses all as one.

BEHAVIOR

The changed state of awareness achieved through Christian meditation not only alters your outlook toward living, but your behavior pattern itself, because the growing awareness of God as one in partnership with you becomes a reality. One man told me that Christian meditation helped him change after years of being a grouch toward his wife and children.

You may experience a new state of consciousness, unconscious peace, and altered personality through Christian meditation. It reorders the unconscious and conscious self with that growing awareness of God in such a way that your attitudes and activities are changed to your good and the honor of God.

I shared this information with Stanley Magee, a student of mathematics. I asked him to diagram the effects of Christian meditation on a scale. His diagram appears on the following page.

The triangle represents everything which makes up you, the person (conscious, unconscious, attitude, personality, moods, temperament, potential, body, spirit, etc.), your activity (job, leisure, relationships, etc.), and requirements for living in our world.

You need to increase your awareness of God at every point of your existence.

The method is Christian meditation.

The result is realization of "total self" under the great Lordship of Jesus Christ.

What is realization of total self?

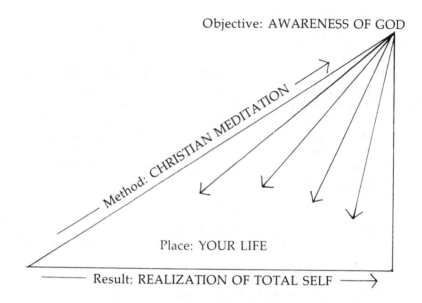

Objective: AWARENESS OF GOD

Method: CHRISTIAN MEDITATION

Place: YOUR LIFE

Result: REALIZATION OF TOTAL SELF

PRIMARILY

POWER TO COPE—TO TAKE CHARGE OF EVENTS AND CIRCUMSTANCES: As the poet Emily Dickinson wrote, "Fate slew him, but he did not drop; she felled, he did not fall / Impaled him on her fiercest stakes, He neutralized them all."

REST FROM STRESS: You may be like the boy who was asked by his father if he were scared. The lad answered, "No, but my stomach is."

RELEASE FROM ANXIETY: Anxiety will make a person "not so much a human being as a civil war," as novelist H. G. Wells wrote.

UNDERSTANDING AND ACCEPTANCE OF YOURSELF: Henry Thoreau correctly stated that as long as a man stands in his own way, everything seems to be in his way. In a similar vein, a doctor told his patient, "I'm afraid you're allergic to yourself."

SECONDARILY, BUT IMPORTANT

Greater peace of mind
Freedom from guilt feelings

Relaxation
Restful sleep
Positive attitudes
Healthy self-love
Genuine happiness
True success
Character improvement
Personality improvement
Patience
Courage
Humility
Enthusiasm
Honesty
Determination
Improved job performance
Stabilized feeling
Greater adaptability
Improved relationships
Sense of hope
Deeply rooted joy
Direction in life
Sense of purpose
Sense of security
Sense of self-worth
Sense of adequacy
Motivation
Life with meaning
Freedom from being used by things to use of things
Self-confidence
Self-control
Victory over depression
Better interaction with others
Enjoyable family life
Freedom to be your own person
Clearer faculties for decision making
Job satisfaction
Harmonious teamwork

Some factors may remain in your life as they were before, but through the practice of Christian meditation, you become more aware of the One who loves and accepts you. You become more conscious of God's nearness and his efficacy in your life.

Such claims sound bold; yet people from all walks of life have discovered that Christian meditation has worked for them. A businessman who completed a seminar could not hide his amazement at the tangible benefits. "I'm at the same company, in the same office, with problems no different than they've been for the past ten years. But what a difference in perspective. I have the power to handle them." A teen-ager confided, "I really am getting along better with Dad." A retired, widowed lady said, "Even though I was a Christian, life was without taste after I lost Sam. What's more, the awareness of God isn't really a new concept to me. I just needed to get the 'how to' of it at this particular time in my life."

Two of the most gratifying demonstrations are from people I shall call Andy and Agnes.

Andy is a prominent businessman and executive in Mississippi. An overachiever, he is a dedicated Christian and a devoted churchman. Now in his forties, Andy has lived a fruitful life, but he felt the need for a down-to-earth way to increase his personal awareness of God. That need led him to a Christian meditation seminar. A few days after he completed the series, he came to my office to share what had happened a few nights previously.

Andy arrived at home late. He was greeted with a letter informing him that he was being audited. An honest person, Andy had nothing to fear, but he had for years been given to immediate and emotional outbursts. He spent almost two hours digging out his receipts and records. In the process, tension increased every minute.

His meditation word for that day was *patience.* Even though I do not suggest that we close the day with a meditation period, Andy's need preempted regular routine. "I got my meditation card," he said, "and had a meditation time. I began to sense God's presence, and, believe it or not, I slept like a baby for the rest of the night." Andy made it clear that in times past he would have fretted, worried, and paced the floor throughout the night.

Agnes was so unsure of herself that she pulled me aside after the introductory lecture of our seminar and asked if I would permit her to attend. She said, "My husband and I run a liquor store. Do you allow such people here?"

Agnes clearly stated that she needed God. "I'm a wreck," she said. From the very first meditation period, her life began to change. It was apparent from her manner. From a demeanor of tension and confusion, she moved to one of peace. "Really," Agnes shared, "I can't believe what's happening to me. It is so unlike me to love God and to believe he is near." In addition, she was surprised by a newly found concern for her family and friends who faced serious problems. The fact that she felt concern enough to think of them and pray for them startled her.

REQUIREMENTS

Through Christian meditation, you advance your state of God-awareness when you deliberately program your thoughts by setting aside specific times each day for meditation. Remember, there is power in repetition. Habitual reinforcement is the key.

This method of increasing your awareness of God is not difficult, but it does have four requirements.

1. COMMITMENT OF WILL

YES, I WILL DO IT. I WILL START.

2. TIME

YES, I WILL ALLOCATE THE TIME TO DO IT.

3. PRACTICE

YES, I WILL FOLLOW THE STEPS INVOLVED IN IT.

4. PERSISTENCE

YES, I WILL KEEP IT UP.

How Important Is Christian Meditation to You?

In this chapter, I want to discuss seven reasons why Christian meditation is very important to you.

STRESS

One reason is the fact that you are exposed to stress daily. Stress results in wear and tear on your body, internal and external strain.

I remember Mike, an optimistic, enterprising man in his thirties who founded a company which manufactured sheet metal ducts used in heating and air-conditioning units. He believed that God was in charge of his life and the power behind his business. His reputation as a conscientious, fair, and reliable man attracted the attention of builders throughout the area. As a result, the business prospered.

Mike was the type of individual who wanted to give his personal attention to all aspects of the operation, but over a period of six to eight years, the sales volume grew to the extent that no single human being could possibly direct everything.

Tension edged in on him. Pressures of the business weighed on him. Relationships and decisions were affected. Mike's appetite declined. The muscles in his back and shoulders actually became so tight that one day he could not turn his neck without turning his entire body. Mike suffered from extreme stress.

Dr. Hans Selye, Professor at the University of Montreal, Canada, and probably the leading medical authority on the subject, calls it "somatic stress," meaning body stress.

Medically, it is "the nonspecific response of the body to any demand made upon it." Stress produces nervousness and hormonal deficiencies. Medical authorities admit to a long list of diseases caused by stress. Those diseases are caused by the person's inappropriate response to the stress.

Among them are:

1. CARDIAC AND CIRCULATORY PROBLEMS

Over half of all deaths in the United States are caused by diseases of the heart and circulatory system.

2. HIGH BLOOD PRESSURE

According to statistics, millions of Americans suffer from high blood pressure. We are bombarded by appeals on radio, TV, and newspapers to have ours checked regularly. It seems to be the legacy of an industrial society.

3. HYPERTENSION

One-third of the American population suffer from hypertension. It is little wonder because hypertension is the child of high blood pressure.

4. STROKES

Strokes, in turn, are caused by high blood pressure and hypertension.

5. GASTROINTESTINAL DISTURBANCES

These disturbances include gastritis, colitis, and ulcers. A physician told me that the states of man in the twentieth century are yes-sir, no-sir, and ul-cer.

Dr. Paul Tournier, the highly respected European physician, claims that we don't die: instead, we kill ourselves with stresses and excesses.

ACCUMULATED STRESS

The problem is compounded when stress is stacked on stress—which appropriately can be called accumulated stress.

This accumulated stress results when there is no relief from stress. The results are frustration, despair, depression, feelings of aimlessness, emptiness, fear, inflexibility, low performance, inefficient living, suspicion, distrust, and disruptions of plans and work. Decision-making processes are slowed down because perception, objectivity, outlook, and assimilation of facts are blurred, for a tired, stressful body leads to a worried and tense mind. In the rush to find at least some temporary respite, we pack doctors' offices and hospital beds. We annually consume over five billion doses of tranquilizers, five billion barbiturates, and three billion amphetamines represented by 200 million prescriptions from physicians.

Resulting sick leave costs industry billions of dollars a year, not to mention the financial loss to individuals for lost work days. There is a drain on personal potential and pride. The feverish search for relief leads to a fanatical quest for frills and thrills. Afterward, as in the use of heroin, a larger dose is required. Tobacco, alcohol, and food become crutches.

Dr. Selye wisely advises that stress is inherent in the activity of life itself. The secret is not to abolish it, but to master it; that is, to live with *stress*, but without *distress!* In addition, we do not achieve freedom from stress by avoiding it. Do you think you can or should remove yourself from every condition that might generate stress? Then you have a formidable task on your hands. To do that would require you to quit living! However, God doesn't call you out of this world. He calls you to become his full person *in* this world.

REST FROM STRESS

A relaxed state of mind will keep you on top of stress and reduce harmful strain to a minimal level. Jesus assured, "I will give you *rest*" (Matt. 11:28, RSV). The Master offered the clue when he stated, "*Take* my yoke upon you, and *learn* from me" (11:29, RSV). The divine invitation is to come, achieve a rested state of mind through the awareness of the presence of God. Christian meditation is a no-nonsense method designed to deal positively with the stress of modern life at its very roots, because it brings a rested state of mind each day.

HAPPIER FAMILY RELATIONSHIPS

Another reason Christian meditation is important to you is because it fulfills the need for happier family relationships. There is disruption in family life throughout the country. The upheaval affects men, women, and children; problems in family relationships also carry over into business and the church.

Statistics show that there are nearly 455 divorces for every 1,000 marriages; 25 percent of all children have only one parent. In 1975, divorces increased by 6 percent over 1974, whereas the number of marriages decreased by 4 percent. Since 1970, the number of households with a female head has jumped by 30 percent.

Even the most rural areas of the nation are feeling these effects. In Mississippi where I pastor a church, the divorce rate over the past ten years has been higher than the national average.

In addition, many families do not go through the formalities of a divorce, but the relationships necessary for meaningful family life are just not there. Couples live a sort of truceful coexistence, an intolerant toleration, and a form void of content. Wedlock has become a deadlock.

This turmoil is not confined to the four walls of the family home. When family problems are persistently ignored and unmanaged, the spillover affects each person in his job, schoolwork, and all his other relationships. For example, when husband and wife have grown indifferent to one another, and love has ebbed out of their lives, they either do not communicate at all, or their contacts are superficial, consisting of trivialities.

Little Tommy and Susie reflect these problems when their schoolwork starts to take a nosedive. They begin to bicker with playmates and their interest in life dwindles. Perhaps their will to cope diminishes.

Dad either slides on the job or throws himself into it in an effort to compensate for his personal and marital conflicts. He is tart and biting toward co-workers; his tolerance level drops significantly, and things which he used to handle efficiently now trip him up. He seems always to be dogged by a nagging tiredness. A few tranquilizers here and there bring him a short-lived respite.

Mom becomes edgy and nervous. When a friend who has confided in her in the past phones and asks for advice, Mom snaps, "What do you think I am, a psychiatrist?" Her pleasure in being with other women is lost. Not knowing exactly the reason, she turns to food, gains forty pounds, and hates herself for it. Her interest in the children's lives and charitable projects slows down, or else she throws herself into these activities recklessly, seeking escape from the war going on inside her.

Mom becomes a super-critical person, finding fault with all and everything. Finally, she thinks, "Oh, I have a physical problem." After a thorough checkup, the doctor breaks the news that nothing of an organic nature seems to be wrong. "Well, I know better," she insists, and she beats a path to the office of one doctor, then another, and another. She may wind up on pills.

Dr. George C. Thosteson, the widely read medical columnist, describes the situation in one of his newspaper articles. He distinguishes between nerve injury or disease and what is too often diagnosed as a case of "nerves." Dr. Thosteson writes:

> True neural ailments are those like Parkinson's disease, Bell's palsy, shingles, sciatica and such. So why the confusion?
>
> It arises because man is often beset by emotional factors—tension, anxiety, fear, love, hate. These, of course, can exist without any physical ailment. But patients turn to doctors with unexplainable headaches ... assorted aches and pains, digestive problems. We know the nervous system controls the various organs and glands, and that these organs can be affected by those emotional factors.

If an outwardly healthy patient complains of symptoms, but examination fails to come up with a physical cause (as, for example, a bowel disease as a cause of constipation) then emotional factors may be suspected. The patient is told, "It's your nerves," or "It's all in your head." That doesn't mean the symptoms aren't real; it's just that the cause may be emotional.

Patients with no obvious ailment may launch long and expensive searches for a doctor to "find" something wrong. They suffer from that chronic all-purpose ailment called "nerves."

Then there are families which endure various disruptions and survive. A little boy revealed his feelings when he told his teacher that his family had moved into a new house. "I love it," he bubbled. "I have my own room. Both of my sisters have rooms. But poor Mom is still in with Dad."

Husband, wife, and children may love one another, but find themselves overwhelmed, or at least seriously threatened, by the pressures of life in today's world.

More "things" with all of their advantages do not offer the solution. Oh, the comforts made possible by an abundant society have their advantages. Remember the millionaire's wife on the television show "Gilligan's Island" who claimed, "Anyone who says that money won't buy happiness doesn't know where to shop"? Money won't secure well-being, but it will finance a research staff to study the problem. As one man told me, "It will make unhappiness a lot more comfortable." The route to personal and family wholeness takes more than things, as Charles W. Colson points out in his book, *Born Again.*

Colson tells of a conversation with Thomas Phillips during the time when Colson was an aide to President Nixon. Mr. Phillips had become executive vice-president of Raytheon Company when he was thirty-seven years of age. By nonstop hard work he became president at age forty. "The success came, all right," said Phillips, "but something was missing. I felt a terrible emptiness. Sometimes I would get up in the middle of the night and pace the floor of my bedroom or stare out into the darkness for hours at a time."

Christian meditation can help you achieve purposeful and enjoyable family life because it gives you qualities needed for fun-filled, meaningful relationships.

RAPID CHANGE

Christian meditation is important to you because of the rapid change taking place in our society. We have been blessed by many aspects of our technology, but we suffer ill effects from it too.

The head of the west coast operation for one of the largest pharmaceutical manufacturers in the world told me that 90 percent of all drugs available today have been developed within the past ten years. Physicians face another serious dilemma. In the time it takes to train a young specialist and get him into practice, much of the information he was taught in medical school is either outdated or has become drastically altered.

According to the lastest statistics, it took man from the beginning of recorded history to the year 1900 to reach a population of one billion. By 1960, population was three billion. In 1976, it exceeded four billion, and if the rate of increase continues, it will reach eight billion by the year 2000. Columnist Henry J. Taylor reported that in the United States a baby is born every eight and one-half seconds; a person dies every seventeen seconds; and an immigrant arrives in the country every sixty seconds. The net increase is one person every fourteen and one-half seconds.

In his book *Future Shock,* Alvin Toffler writes about the inability of the human body to withstand such constantly accelerating changes. We are called upon to receive and assimilate more information in a few months than our forefathers did in a lifetime. Mr. Toffler defines *Future Shock* as the shattering stress and disorientation that we induce in individuals by subjecting them to too much change in too short a time.

Remember the young housewife I mentioned in chapter one?

In addition to her struggles as a new Christian, her family had to move; she started a new job; then the family was faced with another move; her husband's bosses placed new demands on him; and the final steps in the adoption of a son faced her—all within a short period of time. It appears to me that God knows what is best for us by giving us a lifetime in which to experience spiritual growth.

Before accepting the pastorate of Central Presbyterian Church in Jackson, Mississippi, I was a minister in California. The huge backyard of the manse was set apart by a magnificent oak tree which towered about 100 feet into the sky. Beautiful branches swept out in all directions. One day I asked a landscape architect the age of the tree. "I'd say," he answered, "that it's about 125 years old." For a moment it astounded me to think that such a towering, gigantic tree was once a tiny acorn. Then I acknowledged that the transformation from seed to tree involved a great deal of time.

My own life made a new turn when I began to realize a vital principle of genuine growth:

> Yard by yard, it's very hard,
> But inch by inch, it's a cinch!

However, we are faced, in most areas of everyday living, with calls for very rapid change. This eventually takes its toll on us spiritually, emotionally, and physically. We experience a sense of dissatisfaction and a feeling of inadequacy.

Christian meditation is a method available to you to equip you to adapt to change. It increases your ability to be flexible, yet firm.

MORE LEISURE TIME

An excess of leisure time is another reason why Christian meditation is important to you. About one person out of six in Western civilization is retired, and this figure is soon approaching 20 percent of the population. In the United States alone, over 22,000,000 persons are over sixty-five years of age. Americans now live a longer life due to advanced medicine, and thus they have more years to live after retirement.

Also, the average work week is shrinking. From 1890-1954, the work week ranged from sixty-five hours a week in the textile industry to forty; and for railroad employees, from 3,900 hours per year to 2,000. In the United States, the average work week in 1870 was sixty-six hours, whereas in 1956 it was forty-one hours. In twenty to thirty years, it may be necessary for only one-third of the population to work four hours each week to satisfy material needs. What will we do with all of our leisure time then?

Increased leisure time has led to more travel, sports, gambling, and eroticism, according to Dr. Paul Tournier in his book, *Learning to Grow Old*. Boredom and neuroses have also set in because we have not adequately handled our newly acquired leisure time.

We stand in need of a new orientation to work and leisure. Work must become an opportunity for us to express ourselves creatively. Leisure must become an opportunity to ease off and to change our pace for creative purposes—a chance to find new direction for our lives.

Christian meditation is the method to deal with leisure time for two reasons: through it you gain a deep appreciation of the time God gives you; and you unleash the power to organize your life and utilize time effectively.

THE "GO-GO CHURCH"

Although I am a minister, I unapologetically suggest that Christian meditation is important to you because of the "go-go church."

Dale Moody, in his book *Spirit of the Living God*, states that "so much modern religion is just more go-go with no glow in it at all. As artificial logs, twirling with the twinkle of a low-watt bulb, are substituted for hickory logs giving forth real warmth and light, so now the 'planned program' takes the place of the spiritual glow that creates zeal and hope."

Unfortunately, some aspects of religion in the twentieth century, as well intentioned as they may be, have helped to *depersonalize* the individual. However, Jesus' emphasis was on the person. He plainly loved people and used things; but the "go-go church" dictates the reverse order: love things and use people.

You notice that I do not necessarily identify the "go-go church" with the large church. There are many splendid advantages to a large congregation. Your sphere of friendship extends basically to fifteen or twenty people anyway. And so with additional ministers, groups, classes, and related activities in a large church, you may still have the advantages of "small church friendliness."

The real issue is depersonalization. It may come about in a large or small church through overemphasis on programs and the almighty organization at the expense of the person. Congregations of all sizes may be torpedoed by this depersonalization.

The church, as essential as it is to the Christian, was never meant to substitute for the personal practice of Christian meditation. Instead, the church is meant to encourage you, assist you, and show you how to develop into the confident person you are meant to become.

Christian meditation is the method by which you, as an individual, achieve a new sense of who you are because the emphasis is on *you* and *God!*

ANXIETY

To the problems of stress, family relationships, rapid change, more leisure time, and the "go-go church," I now add anxiety.

Anxiety is apprehension and uneasiness—a vague anticipation of danger. The cause of the fear may be unknown or unrecognized; therefore, it causes greater distress. This disagreeable feeling is usually accompanied by a sensation; for example, nervousness, a gut-level feeling of hopelessness, or tense muscles. Anxiety is a sense of pressure which, to some extent, creates a mental disturbance. Anxiety becomes demonstrated as agitation, restlessness, feelings of tautness, dread, and panic.

Dr. Lucien Bovet once said that anxiety finds its sustenance in the painful events of the past (for example, a bad experience), its occasion in some physical weakness in the present (one's response to the past), and its specificity in fear of the future (one wonders, "What will happen to me from this time on?").

The root word is *anxius*, which means to trouble and to choke. Hugh Blair once called anxiety the poison of human life. John Lubbock, noted for his expertise in personnel relations, stated that we often hear of people breaking down from overwork, but in nine cases out of ten, they are really suffering from anxiety. Speaking from long experience, a doctor warns that the person who is unduly influenced by the commonplace events of his day—upset to the point of anger by the gossip of the man at the gas station, roused to fear by his boss, apprehensive about the future—is courting sickness. Dr. Gary Collins, a Christian psychologist, claims that anxiety is the official emotion of our age. In the *Encyclopedia of Mental Health* (1963), we are told that the twentieth century is more anxiety ridden than any other era in history since the Middle Ages.

A short time ago, the findings of some trustworthy researchers at the Medical College of Pennsylvania were reported. To the surprise of many, they found that the suicide rate among American women physicians was three times that of women in general. Among male physicians, the rate was 1.15 times higher than men in general. Why such failure among members of a profession who enjoy income in excess of $50,000 annually, who have the highest social standing in the community? The answer is that they are victims of anxiety produced by the pressures of their life and their response to those pressures.

Anxiety causes mixed feelings inside every one of us, two of which are love and hate. A case in point is the upset young woman who wrote her boyfriend, "Dear Fred: I hate you. Love, Patty." This anxiety leads to confusion and a distorted perception. Doctors Alfred M. Freedman, Harold J. Kaplan, and Benjamin J. Sadock, in *Modern Synopsis of Psychiatry*, claim that whether or not you suffer from anxiety depends on your resources, defenses, and coping mechanism.

CAUSES OF ANXIETY

What are some of the causes of anxiety?

Rejection: *There is within the person a deep need to be accepted. When that need is not filled, he has a feeling of being shunned. Consequently, he experiences anxiety.*

Insecurity: *People want the sense of well-being that comes from having enough to at least take care of the necessities of life. Insecurity resulting in anxiety occurs when there is not a sense of well-being.*

Low self-worth: *"Am I important as a person?" is the question. Everyone needs self-esteem, a vestige of worth as a person. And he needs to feel that there is a kernel of importance to him.*

Loss of love: *The person wonders, "Does anyone really love me for who I am?" "Is there anybody who truly appreciates me?"*

Alienation: *In a society on wheels, people are increasingly isolated from family and close friends. Familial sources of emotional support and affirmation of the worth of individuals worked well in previous generations, but the picture has drastically changed. Thus, people suffer from a sense of alienation.*

Conflict: *Turmoil between husband and wife, parents and children, boss and employee contributes to the problem.*

Frustration: *Such feelings as, "No matter what I try, it turns out wrong," or such feelings as, "I'm prevented from being myself," and "I'm prevented from trying," arise out of frustration.*

Lack of creative expression: *The cry is, "I want to be constructive and to do something that shows the innermost 'me.' "*

Lack of recognition: *A person longs to be recognized; to have appreciation not only for what he does, but for who he is. Recognition gives him a sense of value.*

Lack of new experiences: *Being confined to the same old monotonous routine day after day stifles the spirit and contributes to anxiety. A person needs to always be planning something new and to find ways to do ordinary things differently. I have mapped out a dozen routes to my office without driving more than one-tenth of a mile out of the way.*

Dissatisfaction: *Immersed in layers of guilt feelings, the person never feels that he is doing enough. He always comes up short and is constantly a step behind. I think of a golfer who always finds something wrong with his shot, even if it is a masterful stroke!*

Hostility: *Unresolved differences lead to hostility. One may think that the whole world in which he lives is opposed to him.*

Loneliness: *It is that debilitating feeling of isolation and "by myselfishness" which tears at one's insides.*

Inadequacy: *Crushed by a sense of helplessness, the person who feels inadequate throws up barriers like, "I can't because..."*

Demands: *He feels that others ask too much of him and that there is no way a human being can possibly bear up under such a load.*

Competition: *It is that exhausting effort to beat out someone else, no matter what the cost, such as parents vying for the affection of their children, children for the affection of parents or a certain parent, and competition for dominance.*

Self-centeredness: *It is preoccupation with oneself, until one's own problems and crises begin to mushroom.*

Fanatical goal-setting: *Setting completely unrealistic and unattainable goals, or setting goals that are impossible to reach in the time allotted.*

Depressed goal-setting: *This is a sense of aimlessness; the person feels there are more possibilities for his life than he is experiencing.*

Christian meditation is a method by which to handle anxiety, because it brings to you the consciousness of One who is greater than you are. Yet, this One has your well-being uppermost in his mind.

GROWING AWARENESS OF GOD

Finally, I believe that Christian meditation is important to you because of its objective—to increase your awareness of God.

For your pure pleasure, God has endowed you with senses such as smell, taste, sight, touch, and hearing. Within, God has blessed you with a capacity to know, touch, hear, and see the divine. Let's call it spiritual "awareness."

To be aware means to be cognizant of, conscious to, and informed. Jesus said, "Follow me, and I will make you fishers of men" (Matt. 4:19, RSV). One way of looking at it is: When you live your life in awareness of God, you stay in the process of becoming all you are meant to be. The apostle Paul enlarged on it when he wrote, "The Lord is the Spirit who gives ... life, and where he is there is freedom ... As the Spirit of the Lord works within us, we become more and more like him" (2 Cor. 3:17, 18, TLB).

Let me point out that there is a striking difference between the *presence* of God and *being aware of* the presence of God. Our lack of awareness does not alter the fact, and the fact is that God is present. This story about an atheist illustrates it:

The atheist went into a schoolroom and wrote on the chalkboard, "God is nowhere." Immediately, a student said, "That's wrong. It should read, 'God is now here.' " That is true. God is now here in life with his people, ready to make our life much more enjoyable and meaningful. You may not feel God's nearness and you may not be aware of his closeness, but that lack of awareness of the presence of God cannot and does not bind the magnificent, majestic God of the universe.

However, lack of awareness does profoundly affect you in your daily life. Let me explain with this story about a couple. A few years after the honeymoon, the husband settled into dull routine. The marriage dropped into a boring relationship. Years later, the husband came alive in his marriage and his wife exclaimed, "For the first time, he really listens to me. I think he cares." The wife had been present throughout the thirteen years of their marriage, yet the husband had just begun to be aware of her.

Awareness of God's presence, or lack of it, has a remarkable effect upon you spiritually, emotionally, and physically. To be conscious of God in the mainstream of everyday living transforms people from victims of life to victors in life. In what ways?

ALIENATION

The awareness of God will effectively combat the gnawing problem of feeling alienated or detached. One woman told me that she once felt as detached as the stub of the ticket after having gone through the turnstile at Disneyland.

As a Christian, you *are* a full member of God's family—the grand household of faith. The awareness of God breaks through the barriers you have set up and makes you conscious of belonging. Such a consciousness of belonging will attract you to people and people to you.

LONELINESS

Loneliness is one of the staggering emotional gaps of modern times. Urbanization and industrialization have thrown people in proximity to one another, but they have not really brought people together. Our society has seen increasing despair due to widespread loneliness.

The awareness of God will bring you a new sense of partnership with God. You will experience in mind and spirit the togetherness you were meant to have. There is no need for you to feel that you are a solo in everyday life. Instead, you need to believe that you have at least one true friend—God—and that you can become increasingly cognizant of that partnership.

INFERIORITY

Feelings of inferiority and inadequacy can nag a person to death. A man said, "I have considered my predicament carefully and I have come to the conclusion that I am weak-minded." Such feelings cast a heavy cloud over every aspiration and keep you from becoming a released, achieving person.

The awareness of God will give you a positive outlook. The affirmation brilliantly stated by Paul will take on fresh and applicable meaning: "I can do all things through Christ which strengtheneth me" (Phil. 4:13). That plague of helplessness will be replaced by a humble assurance that you are girded, reinforced, and energized by the One with whom all things are possible. At the same time, you will develop a sense of true humility. It is the art of thinking honestly of yourself, how big and good your God is, how great you are as a child of God, and how you can progress as a person with all your rights and privileges as a member of the divine family.

The awareness of God will increase in you the feeling of unity with God, yourself, others, life, and all of God's creation.

Christian meditation sets loose your awareness of God because it brings to you a new and healing sense of his nearness.

In conclusion, I put to you a question which must be faced: Are Christians truly confronted with stress, the need for happier family relationships, rapidly changing times, more leisure time, the "go-go church," anxiety, and the need for a growing awareness of God?

I should like to answer the question with a question: Do Christians live in a real, down-to-earth world? A physician who attended one of my seminars said, "I used the phrase 'lack of faith' in describing people with stress, tension, and anxiety. But I have come to the conclusion that 'lack of faith' isn't an accurate description, because every day Christians come to my office with the same problems that non-Christians have." Jesus makes the situation plain in his great prayer: "I do not pray that thou shouldst take them out of the world, but that thou shouldst keep them from the evil one" (John 17:15, RSV).

Christian meditation is important to *you*. This book is your invitation to a new wholeness, happiness, and adventure—for people who do, indeed, live in a real, down-to-earth world.

Basic Equipment and Grass Roots Elements of Christian Meditation 4

Christian meditation is not really hard when you set your will to do it. In the back of this book, you will find 124 "Words for the Day." These may be cut out and mounted on cardboard to make them more durable. But you may want to practice Christian meditation on a do-it-yourself basis.

Equipment you will need:

1. BIBLE

Use the translation or paraphrase with which you are most comfortable. I like to use one with modern language.

2. BIBLE CONCORDANCE

This will make it possible for you to find specific verses in the Bible.

3. DICTIONARY

An abridged, paperback copy will do the job. You will need it to look up definitions.

4. SMALL CARDS

You will use these when you write down your Word for the Day. I use 3" × 5" cards.

5. PEN

You need something with which to write.

Now you have the basic equipment to begin this great adventure.

What are the other factors involved in practicing Christian meditation?

TIME

One is time. In the chapter "What Is Christian Meditation?" I mentioned that you increase God-awareness when you deliberately program your thoughts by setting aside times for meditation each day. You will need to arrange these according to the demands of your own schedule. The Psalmist said, "Evening, and morning, and at noon, will I pray" (55:17). To master the art of Christian meditation, you must make the time for it. When a person feels he does not have the time, that is when he most needs to make the time.

I recommend that you begin with a fifteen minute meditation period each day. To do this, go over the schedule you keep on the average day and pick out the period that blends in most acceptably with your schedule. Designate that period of time for Christian meditation. Block it out just as definitely as you would an appointment with the doctor or a client.

For me, it has been most helpful to make my period early in the day, soon after I wake up. But I am a fast riser. When I awake, I am really awake. Others are slow risers—they get up, but they do not wake up until another hour has passed!

It is advantageous, however, to set your meditation period as close to the beginning of your day as possible because it is the time when you point yourself in the direction that you will follow throughout your conscious day.

You may want to meditate during a coffee break or at lunch time. Or perhaps after the children have gone to school. A salesman can meditate while he is waiting to see a client. You may be waiting to see the doctor. I know an executive who tells his secretary that he is in conference. (And he is ... with his God!) This man closes the door to his office and meditates. You may find it necessary to begin with less than fifteen minutes a day; possibly five minutes. It is vital that you begin! Therefore, begin where you are.

Let me suggest that in making time for meditation, you take into account the fact that your energy level varies throughout the day. There are times of greater mental alertness and receptivity. Often these are earlier in the day and before meals. Immediately following a meal, less oxygen is flowing through the brain. The physical processes are geared to digestion; therefore, you are prone to be drowsy. For effective meditation, why not take advantage of natural energy levels, alertness, and receptivity, and avoid times when you must struggle in order to think.

BEDTIME

I recommend that you do not meditate at bedtime unless you have significant reason to do it. Instead, reserve four to five minutes at the very close of your conscious day to give God thanks for the pleasures, opportunities, and responsibilities of that day; to admit before him your failures of that day; to receive his forgiveness; and to release yourself and your loved ones into God's hand. How beautiful it is to go to sleep with thoughts of praise and worship. In the words of the Psalmist, "I trust in thee, O Lord, I say, 'Thou art my God.' My times are in thy hand" (31:14, 15, RSV).

WORD PRINCIPLE

Words reflect feelings and words have sounds. Sounds also show feeling. Suppose a person feels angry and he shouts, "Shut up!" Both the words and the sound of those words have shown his feeling of anger. At the times when you have said, "I love you," the words and the sound of the words showed the love you felt. In Christian meditation the word and its sound will help you to receive what the word means.

It is vital that you use words which can help you to experience a positive feeling; words which will help fill a need that you have at that particular time; or words which represent a quality which you want during that specific day.

I think of it as the "word principle." Every sunrise offers you a new Word for the Day. Examples:

Abundance	*Gladness*
Calmness	*Happiness*
Cheerfulness	*Success*
Energy	*Vitality*
Forgiveness	

The number of possible words is almost unlimited. A businessman who completed my seminar stated that he finds it most helpful to choose a brief word which has a soft sound and which is easy to pronounce.

On the do-it-yourself basis, you will need to invest about five minutes of your meditation period each morning in choosing a Word for the Day. Of course, you may keep the word which you used yesterday. That depends on your need and desires.

POSITION

To get the most out of Christian meditation, you need to settle in a comfortable and unstrained position. Perhaps you will find it most relaxing to kneel, or sit up erect, or lean back in a chair. Consistency has its function; therefore, decide on a position that you will use from day to day.

Keep in mind that the position should not distract your thoughts and that a tense body makes a tense mind. By relaxing the body, you help create a mental environment that is receptive and alert to God's presence and power.

RELAXATION

In his best-selling book, *The Relaxation Response,* Dr. Herbert Benson refers to four basic elements which help to bring on relaxation.

> 1. *A quiet, calm environment with as few distractions as possible.*
> 2. *Use single-syllable words as the contact mental stimulus.*

3. *Take a passive attitude—distracting thoughts should be disregarded.*
4. *Sit comfortably.*

Christian meditation will in turn help you develop a deeper sense of relaxation, but it is important initially that you relax your body for your meditation period. The object here is to release yourself from a rigid body and tightened muscles.

BODY RELAXATION EXERCISE

1. *Select a comfortable position. I suggest that you sit in a chair and loosen any clothes that bind you.*
2. *Let your hands drop to your sides.*
3. *Shake them loosely. Relax. Rest a moment.*
4. *Raise your hands above your head. Stretch them high as though you are reaching for a star. Hold them there and count to five. Let your hands fall to your side. Relax. Rest a moment.*
5. *Raise and drop your eyebrows in an up and down motion. Do this five times. Relax. Rest a moment.*
6. *Press your eyes shut as tightly as possible. Keep them shut for a count of five. Relax. Rest a moment.*
7. *Turn your head to the right as far as possible without moving your shoulders. Hold for a count of five. Now look straight ahead. Relax. Rest a moment.*
8. *Turn your head to the left as far as possible without moving your shoulders. Hold for a count of five. Look straight ahead. Relax. Rest a moment.*
9. *Press your chin to your chest. Go as far as you possibly can. Hold for a count of five. Relax. Rest a moment.*
10. *Lift your shoulders as though you are touching your ears with them—all the way up. Hold for a count of five. Relax. Rest a moment.*
11. *Stiffen your back by sitting up as straight as you possibly can. Arch your back. Hold for a count of five. Relax. Rest a moment.*
12. *Take a deep breath. Slowly inhale. As you hold it for a*

> *count of five, tighten up your stomach as if someone is about to hit you there. Relax. Rest a moment. Repeat this breathing exercise and breathe through your nose, unless some physical condition prevents you from doing so.*
>
> 13. *Tighten your torso. Hold for a count of five. Relax. Rest for a moment.*
> 14.. *Straighten your legs and lift them to the level of your chair. Stretch hard. Tighten up your thighs. Hold for a count of five. Relax. Rest a moment.*
> 15. *Put your feet flat on the floor and press your toes down as far as you can. Hold for a count of five. Relax. Rest a moment.*
> 16. *Now, with feet flat on the floor, point your toes up toward your head. Stretch them upward. Hold for a count of five. Relax. Rest a moment.*
> 17. *Be completely still. Enjoy your newly relaxed body. When you are ready to go about other duties, move slowly at first. There is no need to rush.*

Obviously, this body relaxation exercise can be used anywhere there is a chair or an elevated seat of some kind. People are using it in the home, in the office, and at other places on the job. A construction worker told me that he uses it during his lunch hour.

Parts of the exercise are usable while driving a car. A salesman commented that when his back begins to tense up, he lifts his shoulders toward his ears a few times, stiffens his back by sitting up straight, takes a few deep breaths, and tightens and releases his torso—all on the interstate. And it really helps him!

Another man said that he has stopped on the side of the highway many times and gone through most parts of the exercise while in his car.

Remember, the Lord has a vested interest in your body as well as your mind and spirit. He gave you a body. It is his will that your body be maintained in good health. Allowing it to become racked with tension is just as wrong as allowing your attitude to be infected with poisonous thoughts.

CONSCIOUS THOUGHT

The idea behind conscious thought is to willfully think about a certain word. By consciously thinking on a single word, you give direction to your thoughts. Over a period of time, you will probably be amazed at the power of thought control which you develop. In Christian meditation, the emphasis is *not* on concentration.

Concentration means to "gang up" your thoughts. Sometimes it is a battle to do that. In fact, it is possible to concentrate so hard on concentrating that you get tense and stressful in your efforts to concentrate. You begin to fight to keep your mind from wandering and the value of meditation is lost.

Instead of seeking concentration, I suggest that by consciously thinking on your word for a few moments, you gently influence your thoughts toward the desired objective. As one man told me, you try to nudge the mind. In that way, the mind is not left to wander to and fro wherever the winds blow it. Since your quest is for a deepening, growing awareness of God's presence, you point your thoughts toward his nearness by use of the word you select for the day. Think of it as mental guidance without struggling.

"But what happens when my thoughts get off track?" asked a young man in one of my seminars. He explained that when he began to meditate, he found his thoughts were apt to drift like Stephen Leacock's rider who "flung himself upon his horse and rode madly off in all directions."

The secret is the word and the use of it. Work on a free and easy flow of your word, from which you immediately move into prayer. When your thoughts wander, which they may do occasionally, bring them back to the word by looking at your card and repeating the word. Then continue in prayer.

USE OF EYES

Bill Gober, a friend of mine who is with the Young Men's Christian Association, told me about a young woman who attended a "Y" congress held on the campus of Miami University,

Ohio. She was a striking young woman from South America. Her smooth tan skin, big beautiful brown eyes, and long, flowing auburn hair set her apart from the crowd. However, her native language was Portuguese. She could not speak any English.

About two days after the congress began, Bill noticed an eighteen-year-old American boy buddying around with her. On the third day, they were holding hands—evidence that the relationship had grown. On the fourth day, they were closer; in fact, each one had an arm around the other.

Bill pulled the young man aside and said, "How in the world are you two managing to get along? She speaks only Portuguese. You speak only English." The fellow replied, "Mr. Gober, her eyes tell me everything I want to hear."

In a sense, the eyes talk. They speak a language of their own.

In Christian meditation, the use of your eyes is helpful as you seek to increase your awareness of God. In the meditation period, it will be advantageous to close them gently and softly. They may flutter some as you begin, but after a few days of meditation, they will settle down.

At the close of the meditation period, you open them to words of praise and gratitude.

MENTAL PICTURES

By using your built-in mental screen, you put to work your God-given powers of imagination.

The word "imagination" is derived from "image." The Bible says, "God created man in his own *image,* in the *image* of God he created him; male and female he created them" (Gen. 1:27, RSV). I believe this means, among other things, that you are endowed with the creative power of imagination. So use it to increase your awareness of God, for *whatever you create, you first imagine.*

In Christian meditation, you use imagination to picture Jesus beside you. You visualize him speaking personally to you, imparting to you what your Word for the Day means. Or, you establish in your mind a scene you have read in the Bible and relate it directly to yourself at the moment. For example:

> *"The Lord is my* shepherd.*"*
>
> *Visualize him as a shepherd showing you the way.*
>
> *"He leads me beside the* still waters.*"*
>
> *Visualize a quiet, still lake.*
>
> *"You are made* whole.*"*
>
> *Think of Jesus standing beside you and touching you.*
>
> *"I will go to my* Father.*"*
>
> *Visualize God as a father acting in love toward you, welcoming you.*
>
> *"I can do all things through Christ who* strengthens me.*"*
>
> *Picture Jesus at your side imparting power to you.*

PRAYER

Prayer is talking to God. As spiritual communication, it is sharing yourself with the Almighty. The basic purpose of prayer is to pull us step by step, increasingly, into the awareness of God. Through prayer we are increasingly brought into a greater sense of God's purpose for us and into a sphere of divine life even while we are on earth.

Olive Wyon put it in understandable terms by saying, "The aim of prayer is not primarily the meeting of the needs of the person praying, but the transformation of the whole life to God's glory."

In Christian meditation it is necessary to give and receive in the exercise of prayer. Give your thoughts to God by sharing them. Since God is vitally interested in you, he is interested in everything which genuinely concerns you.

Some thoughts you share with God during your meditation may rise from your unconscious mind and surface in your conscious mind. These thoughts may represent hidden, repressed fears or aspirations, or perhaps some feelings acquired from childhood experiences. They could very well be feelings caused by scars from the past. Let me say it once more. Share your thoughts with God because your search for greater awareness depends on it.

Prayer is receiving as well as giving. Therefore, in meditation, let God know that you wish to grow in understanding and to receive the benefits of your Word for the Day. Then thank him, because *gratitude* grows a wonderful *attitude*.

PRAYER MOMENTS

Would it be natural for partners in a marriage relationship to speak to one another only at scheduled times? Of course not. Then neither is it normal for you to pray only during your meditation period. For that reason, it is important in your quest for a deeper awareness of God to take prayer moments throughout the day. Use short, sentence prayers—"flash prayers," as Dr. Frank Laubach called them.

You can train your mind to pray at specific times. Examples:

When you open a door.
When you unlock a door.
When you lock a door.
When you close a door.
When you get out of the car.
When you get in the car.
When you pass a grocery store.
When you drive by a church.
While you are waiting for an appointment.
While you wait at a traffic signal.
When you wash your hands.
When you drink a glass of water.
When you wash the dishes.
While you iron the clothes.
When you hear the doorbell.

I know of a man who made a mark on the face of his watch so that each time he looked at it, he would be prompted to pray.

MEDITATION CUES

A cue is a signal to point you in a certain direction; it prepares you for something which is to follow.

At the beginning of each meditation period, I use a cue. My favorite is Psalm 46:10 (RSV).

Be STILL,

and

KNOW

that I am

GOD.

This assurance from the Word of God gives me confidence that my heavenly Father wants me to know him, and that knowledge is a sure-fire result of a growing awareness of God. It also tells me that I am to be still—in body and spirit—so that I can better absorb the awareness of God's presence.

In addition, I make use of four other cues occasionally.

Isaiah 40:31

THEY that

WAIT

upon the

LORD

shall RENEW

their STRENGTH;

they shall mount up with wings as

eagles; they shall run and not be

weary; and they shall walk, and

not faint.

By that cue, I am assured that God renews my strength when I take the time to draw on the limitless reservoir he offers me.

Isaiah 26:3 (RSV)

Thou dost

KEEP

him in perfect

PEACE

whose mind is stayed

on thee.

What a peaceful guarantee that cue is to me! Of course, the way to peace of mind is very clear: "... whose *mind* is stayed on thee." A paraphrase forcefully points out the meaning: "... whose thoughts turn often to the Lord" (TLB).

Romans 8:31, 32 (RSV)

If

GOD

IS FOR US,

who is against us?

He who did not spare

his own Son but gave

him up for us all,

will he not also

GIVE

US

ALL

THINGS

with him?

To me, that is God's pledge of whose side God is on. He is *for* me and he *gives* me all things. In recognizing his lordship as the great Giver of all things, I am released from a dominance by things, to an enjoyment of things.

Philippians 4:19 (RSV)

My

GOD

will

SUPPLY

every need of yours

according to his

riches in glory in

Christ Jesus.

As a cue, this verse conditions me to the commitment God makes in offering his total resources to fill my need. He will supply the answer which is best for me.

It will be helpful for you to memorize these five meditation cues and to use one of them at the beginning of each meditation.

Once more, the basic equipment you need to practice Christian meditation on a do-it-yourself basis is:

Bible
Bible concordance
Dictionary
Small cards
Pen

The grass roots elements involved in Christian meditation are:

Time
Words
Position
Relaxation
Conscious thought
Use of eyes
Mental pictures
Prayer
Meditation cues

LET'S GO!

I asked a woman her reason for enrolling in my Christian Meditation Seminar. She responded, "To find how I can really shut out the world and its distractions and think on God."

This is a how-to book and there is no substitute for starting. So let's get going by taking the necessary steps for Christian meditation.

1. SELECT YOUR WORD FOR THE DAY

Choose a word (either your own or one from the back of this book) that demonstrates a need or aspiration you have and one that can generate a positive feeling. If you have selected your own, write it in big capital letters on your meditation card and use the dictionary to define it.

You may spend about five minutes selecting your word, writing it on your meditation card, and looking up its definition. Example:

PEACE

Definition: A state of tranquillity; freedom from mental agitation, fear, and anger; harmony.

John 14:27—Peace I [Jesus] leave with you, my peace I give unto you ... Let not your heart be troubled, neither let it be afraid.

---

2. GET IN POSITION

Get comfortable and relaxed. To help, use the body relaxation exercise outlined in chapter four.

3. REPEAT YOUR MEDITATION CUE

I recommend that you repeat it two or three times: Psalm 46:10, or Isaiah 40:31, or Isaiah 26:3, or Romans 8:31, 32, or Philippians 4:19.

4. CONSCIOUS THOUGHT

Look at your word on the card, for it now serves as a symbol, an aid, a reminder, and a prompter. Read the definition once or twice, pausing to consider the definition. You should not be in a hurry, so read the definition slowly.

Read the Bible verse of assurance which is related to your word, but remember that haste makes waste. Let your reading pace be like a leisurely stroll. You want to let the truth God offers through the verse soak into your mind and spirit. You will not fully experience it if you are rushed.

Begin to think your word.
Begin to say it silently.
Do so until you say it without effort. Let the word flow freely.
It may be of value to speak it audibly at first, then soften the sound each time you say the word. Example:

PEACE
PEACE
Peace
Peace
peace

Possibly, you are repeating your word in rhythm with your breathing.

Inhale: Peace
Exhale: Peace

You are now repeating it in silence. If your thoughts begin to wander, relax and bring them back to the word by looking at it and reading the meditation verse.

5. CLOSE YOUR EYES

Close your eyes gently and softly—not tightly. Relax them as you repeat your word. The muscles of your eyelids may be wound up; therefore they might flutter upon closing at first. As I have said, they will settle down after a few days of meditation.

Closing your eyes has purpose. It has the effect of putting you and God in direct communication, one-on-one.

6. MENTAL PICTURES

With eyes gently closed, visualize on the movie screen of your mind Jesus Christ bringing to *you* that which your word demonstrates.

Example: Peace. You picture the peace-giving Christ standing beside you, reaching out, placing his hands upon your head or shoulders, and speaking "Peace" to you. Visualize yourself responding, "Yes, I accept your peace."

7. PRAYER

At this moment in your meditation, begin to share every thought with God. Prayer is conversing with God. Do not hold back anything. Do not consider any thought as trite, petty, or insignificant, because God is interested in you as a whole person.

Maybe some thoughts you have at this time in your meditation are rising to the surface of your conscious mind. They may represent hidden, repressed, suppressed, or oppressed experiences in your life from days past: fears, feelings, hopes, and ambitions. Let God heal these thoughts.

Prayer is receiving as well as giving.

Then express your thankfulness to God. I repeat: gratitude leads to a wonderful attitude. Speak words of praise to him.

8. OPEN YOUR EYES

Open them slowly, and as you do, continue words of thankfulness. "I am glad, loving God, that you have now given me peace."

Pause for a few moments to reflect on your experience with God during the meditation period.

Let the triumph come through!

Do not fence in your newly found awareness of God.

TIME

I have recommended a fifteen-minute meditation period each day. May I also suggest that you use an alarm or some other device to remind you when the fifteen minutes are over. You may find the experience as stimulating as one businessman did—he was late to his office four mornings consecutively.

USE OF THE MEDITATION CARD

Let's get back to the meditation card. It can be a resourceful reminder to you throughout the entire day, so take it with you and post it at places where you can glance at it occasionally. You can use it at key moments such as when you tend to get agitated, upset, tense, worried, and when there is good news or bad news.

You may want a different meditation card for each day of the year. Or you may want to use the same card for two days, a week, two weeks. You may select a few basic words which represent needs or aspirations and use them exclusively. Example: Thirty words on thirty cards for thirty days, after which you start over with a new set.

Tailor your pattern to best meet your need in mastering Christian meditation.

Objective:
TO INCREASE YOUR AWARENESS OF GOD IN ALL OF YOUR LIFE.

Fringe benefit:
Greater realization of your total self.

CHRISTIAN MEDITATION GROUPS

For many people, another key to continuing growth in Christian meditation is to meet in small groups where there is mutual sharing and support. I recommend that you get a meditation group started in your church, neighborhood, club, or business.

HOW MANY PEOPLE?

Even three or four members are sufficient; but a group of ten to twelve is large enough to make the experience interesting, yet, small enough to keep it personal. *To get underway, you need only three or four.* Bring them together, discuss the idea, and decide on the next meeting. You are on the way!

LEADERSHIP

General George S. Patton, Jr., of World War II fame, is reported to have said that, whether it is a piece of spaghetti or a military unit, there is only one end from which to lead it: the front end. This is true of the Christian meditation group.

The leader makes the difference! You need at least one person committed to increasing his awareness of the presence of God with a group. Shared responsibility will work for the group, but it still must begin with one committed person.

The leader is responsible for group meetings—reminding members of those meetings and their location. He may delegate these jobs, but he should see that they get done. He should also have access to a cassette recorder and the Christian Meditation cassette tape to use at least at first (see back of book).

CHRISTIAN MEDITATION MATERIALS

In this chapter, Christian meditation material to get your group started is suggested. If you choose to use materials from our office in starting your group, the Christian Meditation Association has packets which contain supplies for twelve meetings. The cost of printing and mailing is $2.00 per packet and each person in the group should have one.

LOCATION

A location for the group is most commonly a home, office, or a meeting room in a church. It should be informal and offer a relaxed setting. The leader helps to build an environment, but the place in which the group meets offers surroundings. *Remember, however, any place is better than no place at all.*

HOST

A host for the group meeting will prove helpful. Of course, the host and the leader may be the same person for awhile. But, as soon as possible, the leader should distribute the responsibility. In that way, more leaders and hosts will be developed. The host accommodates the group for its meeting and prepares refreshments.

THREE IMPORTANT WORDS

There are three very important words for the meditation group. One is PERSONAL. The importance of the individual before God is to be emphasized at all times. Another is PARTICIPATE. The benefits derived from the meditation group are directly proportionate to the honest and willing participation of those in the group. But *do not force participation.* The third word is PERSONS: others. Although each person in the meditation group is there as an individual, he is also there to help others in the group: to share, support, encourage, and pray for the others.

OUTLINE FOR CHRISTIAN MEDITATION GROUP

Informal sharing
Meditation affirmation
Inspirational-devotional
The Lord's Prayer
Christian meditation
Prayers of concern
Closing thought

Sample:

CHRISTIAN MEDITATION GROUP MEETING

INFORMAL SHARING

Those in attendance may discuss past experiences they have had during Christian meditation; or the reason they are in this group and have come to this particular meeting; or hopes they hold for their own lives through Christian meditation.

CHRISTIAN MEDITATION AFFIRMATION

To be read in unison, then individually, silently, and slowly. When reading individually, personalize the assurance by substituting "I," "me," or "my" for any other personal pronoun.

> Group: "In quietness and in confidence shall be your strength" (Isa. 30:15).
> Personalize: In quietness and in confidence shall be my strength.

CHRISTIAN MEDITATION DEVOTIONAL

"God's Healing Power"
Long ago, some intelligent thinker wrote:

> He who formed our frame,
> Made man a perfect whole;
> And made the body's health
> Depend upon the soul.
> (Source Unknown)

Those lines ring with a certain truth which is supported by the Greatest Book in the world. The Psalmist left to all people his own wonderful experience when he wrote: "O Lord my God, I cried to thee for help, and thou hast healed me" (Psa. 30:2, RSV). Then another of God's champions claimed: "But for you who fear [reverence] my name the sun of righteousness [God] shall rise with healing in its wings" (Mal. 4:2, RSV).

Back to the Psalmist. He speaks of the Triple Crown of divine involvement in these words: "[God] forgives all your iniquity ... heals all your diseases ... redeems your life from the Pit" (Psa. 103:3, 4, RSV). This means that God pushes away our wrongs; God pulls us together in health; and God puts us into life with the power, zest, and victory for abundant living.

There is still more.

Of Jesus Christ it was said: "He himself took our illnesses and carried away our diseases" (Matt. 8:17, TEV). Luke in his

Gospel witnesses to this Galilean placing his hands on the people and healing them (Luke 4:40). John opens his third letter by saying, "I pray that everything may go well with you, and that you may be in good health" (v. 2, TEV).

Is it not unmistakably clear that the heavenly Father cares about every whit and bit of our existence—including our health? His love is for the total person—soul, mind, and body. But the effect of his care is nullified, as it pertains to us, unless we believe and accept it.

We are assured that:

God loves us.

As complete persons, we are important to him.

God can do anything.

God has healing power.

God's healing power is ours.

THE LORD'S PRAYER

Repeat it thoughtfully and in unison.

> Our Father, who art in heaven,
> Hallowed be thy name.
> Thy kingdom come.
> Thy will be done on earth as it is in heaven.
> Give us this day our daily bread.
> And forgive us our debts,
> as we forgive our debtors.
> And lead us not into temptation,
> but deliver us from evil:
> For thine is the kingdom,
> and the power,
> and the glory,
> forever.
> Amen.

CHRISTIAN MEDITATION

Meditate five to fifteen minutes. The group may meditate together using a common word, or each one may choose his own word. Or those in attendance may meditate privately. If this is the case, let each one think of himself as alone in the room.

PRAYERS OF CONCERN

Pray for each other by name and need. Keep a prayer list for people not in the group and update it at each meeting. Before prayer, repeat an appropriate verse or affirmation. For example:

> Let your power, Lord,
> flow through us to help
> one another.

CLOSING THOUGHT

As a group, repeat Psalm 23.

Because the Lord is my Shepherd, I have everything I need!

He lets me rest in the meadow grass and leads me beside the quiet streams.

He restores my failing health.

He helps me do what honors him the most.

Even when walking through the dark valley of death I will not be afraid, for you are close beside me, guarding, guiding all the way.

You provide delicious food for me in the presence of my enemies.

You have welcomed me as your guest; blessings overflow!

Your goodness and unfailing kindness shall be with me all my life, and afterwards I will live with you forever in your home (Psalm 23, TLB).

LET'S TALK ABOUT IT

Discuss feelings and results of this Christian meditation time.

SELECT A DISCIPLINE FOR THE WEEK

In Christian meditation, you must be open to positive change. Choose a discipline for the week.

1. Affirm God's closeness by realizing throughout the day that God is now with you, even standing beside you. Short sentence prayers during the day will help you to be aware of God's nearness.

2. Start affirming your importance as a person whom God has created and loves. A whole person—body, mind, and spirit. If in need of better health, use Psalm 103:3-5; or Luke 18:27, three times daily.

3. Replace one negative habit with a positive habit. Habit is the result of repetition. The way to eliminate an undesirable habit is to get going with a wholesome habit.

4. In prayer every day, ask that an unwholesome or negative feeling (for example, fear, anxiety, inferiority, hate, resentment) be replaced by faith, hope, and love.

CHRISTIAN MEDITATION GROWTH CHART

One of the most helpful things a person can do is to think about what he has accomplished and record the results. Certainly that is the case in the practice of Christian meditation.

I suggest that you keep a growth chart of your feelings and experiences, day by day, for at least the next thirty days. It takes only a few minutes to use the growth chart, and the rewards can be great.

Another reason for the chart is that you may need additional help. The following chapters can assist you, but the chart will indicate what kind of encouragement you need.

The chart includes room for one meditation period. Below the day, specify the date, then the time of your meditation.

Example
Sunday
June 20
7:30-7:45 A.M.

CHRISTIAN MEDITATION GROWTH CHART

Date	Word	Meditation verse	What happened during your meditation?	What difference did it make during the day?
Sunday				
(Date)				
(Time)				
Monday				
(Date)				
(Time)				
Tuesday				
(Date)				
(Time)				
Wednesday				
(Date)				
(Time)				
Thursday				
(Date)				
(Time)				
Friday				
(Date)				
(Time)				
Saturday				
(Date)				
(Time)				

CHRISTIAN MEDITATION GROWTH CHART

Date	Word	Medi-tation verse	What happened during your meditation?	What difference did it make during the day?
Sunday				
(Date)				
(Time)				
Monday				
(Date)				
(Time)				
Tuesday				
(Date)				
(Time)				
Wednesday				
(Date)				
(Time)				
Thursday				
(Date)				
(Time)				
Friday				
(Date)				
(Time)				
Saturday				
(Date)				
(Time)				

CHRISTIAN MEDITATION GROWTH CHART

Date	Word	Meditation verse	What happened during your meditation?	What difference did it make during the day?
Sunday				
(Date)				
(Time)				
Monday				
(Date)				
(Time)				
Tuesday				
(Date)				
(Time)				
Wednesday				
(Date)				
(Time)				
Thursday				
(Date)				
(Time)				
Friday				
(Date)				
(Time)				
Saturday				
(Date)				
(Time)				

CHRISTIAN MEDITATION GROWTH CHART

Date	Word	Medi-tation verse	What happened during your meditation?	What difference did it make during the day?
Sunday				
(Date)				
(Time)				
Monday				
(Date)				
(Time)				
Tuesday				
(Date)				
(Time)				
Wednesday				
(Date)				
(Time)				
Thursday				
(Date)				
(Time)				
Friday				
(Date)				
(Time)				
Saturday				
(Date)				
(Time)				

CHRISTIAN MEDITATION GROWTH CHART

Date	Word	Medi-tation verse	What happened during your meditation?	What difference did it make during the day?
Sunday				
(Date)				
(Time)				
Monday				
(Date)				
(Time)				
Tuesday				
(Date)				
(Time)				
Wednesday				
(Date)				
(Time)				
Thursday				
(Date)				
(Time)				
Friday				
(Date)				
(Time)				
Saturday				
(Date)				
(Time)				

Indicate the word you are using that day and the meditation verse. Immediately following your meditation, write down your feelings. Of course, you will want to be totally honest. It is important that you do this as soon as you finish your meditation.

Near the close of the day, reflect for a moment on experiences you had during the day.

Was there a difference?

Write it down in concise form.

Included are enough pages for five weeks. You may not want to continue the chart indefinitely, but for the first thirty days it can be a valuable help in your practice of Christian meditation.

The next four chapters will deal with the positive benefits you can receive from Christian meditation.

Correctly practiced, Christian meditation will:

Release to you the energy you need to resolve guilt feelings.

Enable you to handle tension.

Give you the desire to tame your temper and creatively redirect your energy.

Enrich your spiritual life so that you will overcome worry.

Get the Edge on Guilt Feelings

5

Read this passage slowly and meditatively

O loving and kind God, have mercy. Have pity upon me and take away the awful stain of my transgressions.

Oh, wash me, cleanse me from this guilt. Let me be pure again.

For I admit my shameful deed—it haunts me day and night.

It is against you and you alone I sinned, and did this terrible thing.

Create in me a new, clean heart, O God, filled with clean thoughts and right desires.

A broken and a contrite heart, O God, you will not ignore.

When my heart is right, then you will rejoice in the good that I do....

(Psalm 51:1-4, 10, 17, 19, TLB)

Unresolved feelings of guilt can become a cancerous force in a person's life, eating away at his insides. They steal away the joy of living by making the person feel confined and repressed.

Dr. Hobart Mowrer, a distinguished doctor, said, "Our greatest and most devastating anguish is experienced, not in physical pain or biological deprivation, but when we feel guilty as a person."

According to another physician who is a friend of mine, people are experiencing more guilt today than ever before. One woman weight-watcher said that she got an awful guilt feeling when she wanted to tear into a luscious, three-layer German chocolate birthday cake, even though it did have artificially sweetened decorations on it.

I have found that it is relevant to ask the following questions of a person who has a sense of guilt:

1. *Are you friendly or hostile?*
2. *Are people attracted to you or do they shy away from you?*
3. *How do you feel when you wake up in the morning–high, low, reckless, cheerful, or grumpy?*
4. *What about one hour after you wake up? Two hours? Three hours? When the day is over?*
5. *What kind of a day do you generally have? "Great," "you-wouldn't-believe-it," or "so-so"?*
6. *How important are you making yourself to your employer? Or do you work just to live?*
7. *Are you polite or rude?*
8. *How happy is your family life?*
9. *How big are your hopes, and how tenacious are you in sticking to them?*
10. *How much of a climber in life are you? Or do you leave the peaks for the younger generation?*
11. *How healthy are you? What about your symptoms of migraines, nervousness, tension, allergies, and ulcers? (Before you scoff them off, consider the experience of a doctor who, in treating over 100 cases of arthritis and colitis, discovered that almost 70 percent of his patients were suffering from a hidden sense of guilt, and that, in his professional judgment, it contributed significantly to their ailments.)*
12. *Are you deliberately clinging to pain and unhappiness?*

Guilt has "her pale tormentor, misery," as William Cullen Bryant so aptly stated it. Like a miserable parasite, guilt feasts on the past. Charles Curtis spoke of guilt as a fear of your past which is blown up by suspicion. As Shakespeare wrote in *King Henry VI*, "Suspicion always haunts the guilty mind; the thief doth fear each bush an officer." Some of the closest friends of guilt are shame, self-pity, inferiority feelings, and anxiety. By considering some philosophies surrounding guilt feelings, we will get a more adequate understanding of them.

One mistaken idea holds that you should never have guilt feelings because you are not actually guilty of anything wrong. According to advocates of this philosophy, people are but victims of circumstances, heredity, environment, stupid laws, and silly regulations.

Another school of thought holds that guilt feelings come when you violate laws of society. Of course, there is truth there, but the mistake occurs when laws of man are thought to be the only standard.

A third philosophy says that guilt is the feeling you have when you offend your own conscience. Naturally, this is true as far as it goes, but what if I were to shoot you and feel no guilt? Would I then be guiltless?

There is still another approach to guilt feelings which claims that they result when you violate the way of God and break the purposes of God for you. When the Psalmist prayed, "O loving and kind God, have mercy ... Oh wash me, cleanse me from my guilt," he sensed an overwhelming guilt. At the same time, he had broken a law of social relationships, offended his own conscience, and transgressed the way of God for him.

I think of a feeling of guilt in these terms: Guilt is the feeling a person has when he knows he has violated a moral or social law, and/or a law which favors his own highest interests.

Let's consider a moral law such as humility. Moments of conceit and cockiness (which are false impressions of yourself and destructive selfishness) bring a sense of spiritual pain. The taboo against stealing is an example of a social law. It is also a moral law for which society prescribes a penalty. Obeying this law favors your own highest interests.

Of course, we must acknowledge that the capacity to sense guilt is conditioned by environment: those closest to you, circumstances, conditions and events which deeply influence you, written laws, and society in general. Yet, there is a higher conditioning. God has given you the ability to know and love him, and to enjoy him always.

That small but powerful inner voice called conscience is involved. However, in the absence of all other forces such as positive environment, favorable circumstances, etc., God is there to arouse that basic sense within you. For instance, something to which the factors of environment, circumstances, written laws, and society in general do not speak still may feel right or wrong to me. That is because my spirit inclines me to accept it as right or wrong. The apostle Paul referred to this force when he spoke of the law within us.

Guilt feelings in their unresolved state generate internal conflict. That conflict is with ourself, others, our conditions, or God—and possibly a combination of all these.

I have used the word "unresolved" to mean that sense of guilt for which the solution has not been accepted and applied. So the elementary question to be answered in this chapter is: How do you resolve the causes of guilt feelings? The secret is much like the solution of alcoholism. The alcoholic is cured when he really gets to the reasons behind his drinking and accepts and applies the answers.

1. ACCEPT RESPONSIBILITY FOR GUILT FEELINGS

Begin by accepting responsibility for your guilt feelings.

I passed a schoolyard just in time to see a ball sail over a chain-link fence. About a dozen children said all together, "I'll get the ball." The teacher in charge said, "Don't all talk at once. Let me choose one responsible child to get the ball." A little fellow answered, "Teacher, I'm responsible. I kicked it over." He probably did not realize it, but he spoke a deep and remarkable truth about responsibility.

Some time ago, a man down on life came to see me. He was as beaten as any person I have ever seen. I said, "You look like you've had it," and he answered, "I have." He told me that his childhood wasn't very happy; that his parents weren't able to send him to the university that he wanted to attend; that his own marriage had been a wreck because of his wife and her family; that his children were alienated from him; and that the straw that broke the camel's back was the loss of his job. In effect, he tried to tell me that he was no longer responsible for what he did or what he was.

I asked if he felt any guilt, and he replied, "None at all. Guilt has no basis when you're not responsible." I reminded my visitor that the one great law of success in any undertaking is to accept responsibility. "A man who refuses to admit his mistakes can never be successful. But if he confesses and forsakes them, he gets another chance" (Prov. 28:13, TLB).

Responsibility for guilt rests predominantly in your own hands and not in heredity, or environment, or luck, or "the way the cookie crumbles"!

Even if conditions have not been or are not as desirable as you wish, it is your response to them that counts. The big turning point begins when you acknowledge, "I am responsible."

Long ago, the Psalmist said it in a way that never goes out of style. "I know my transgressions, and my sin is ever before me" (51:3, RSV).

2. AVOID THE GUILT FEELINGS OF OTHERS

Another important step toward release is to avoid borrowing the guilt of others.

Other people, out of a sense of guilt, may consciously or unconsciously try to impose their ideas and convictions on you. If you act as a doormat and accept their views without thought, study, and prayer, you may begin to share their guilt complex. When that happens, their feelings of guilt have been passed on to you.

I listened to a nationally known educator as he pointed this out. During a visit to a New Jersey school, he found that of twenty-five six-year-old students in one class, eleven were on tranquilizers, yet they were not considered problem children. They were normal, all-American, everyday, first-grade boys and girls. The educator remarked, "I asked myself, What is so distressing in the world of a six-year-old that requires him to be on barbiturates?" He discovered that the parents were heavily into pills and that the children only reflected the feelings of apprehension and guilt possessed by the parents.

Now, I am aware that they were only youngsters and that at their age, they only knew how to accept what parents passed on to them. However, borrowing guilt is possible, whatever your age and relationship to others.

God has given you a mind to think.

He has equipped you with feet to stand on.

He gave you the faculty of choice.

You need to think, stand on your feet, and use the power of choice.

You can and need to listen to others. You need others, but ultimately you must decide for yourself.

It is interesting to me that the Psalmist owned up to only *his* guilt—not the guilt of other individuals or of the world at large. In that way, he avoided the guilt feelings of others.

3. TAKE GUILT FEELINGS TO GOD

The third step is to take your guilt feelings to God. As Dr. Donald Cole once said to my congregation, "Guilt is the feeling you have when you are estranged from God."

I already mentioned that guilt is the sense you possess when you violate God's way. That feeling of guilt continues when forgiveness is unaccepted and unapplied, but God offers forgiveness and another chance.

I was once told about a young man who had a selfish life at home. Thinking that he knew everything there was to know, he wondered how it could be possible for his father to be as old as he was, yet so ignorant.

One day the young man packed a few clothes in a suitcase and ran away, promising that to his dying day he would never return. "I'll show them," he assured himself.

But the world did not treat him as kindly as he had hoped it would. Since he was only a teen-ager, he could not find a job. He ate meagerly, stretching what little money he had as far as he could. But soon the money was used up and he began exchanging odd jobs for meals.

In desperation, the young man wrote to his father and asked his forgiveness. He told his father that he wanted to come home, and that on a certain day he would be on the train that stopped at the little town. "If you forgive me," wrote the son, "hang a towel on the gate in front of our house. I'll see it when the train passes by. If there is no towel, I won't get off the train. I'll keep going."

As the train approached the town, the young man nervously looked out the window. He paced up and down the aisle, shuffling his duffle bag from hand to hand. As the train rounded the curve not far from the house, the young man asked a friend to look for him. "I'm afraid to," he confessed.

As the train passed the house, his friend looked. He turned to the young man and said, "Look for yourself." The teen-ager slowly turned his head. He saw a big white towel hanging on the gate, and towels and sheets blowing in the breeze from every limb of every tree. He leaped off the train and ran to his father who was waiting in front of the fence.

God is like that father. The Psalmist prayed, "Against thee, thee only, have I sinned.... Purge me ... and I shall be clean; wash me, and I shall be whiter than snow. Create in me a clean heart, O God, and put a new and right spirit within me" (51:4, 7, 10, RSV). And God responded in forgiveness.

Take your guilt feelings to God. Present them to the Lord as you would to a trusted friend. Mention your desire to be forgiven and believe that you are forgiven from that moment. Accept forgiveness as a reality and thank God.

Any time the old guilt tries to rear its ugly head, speak authoritatively to it, "God has forgiven me. You're dead as far as I am concerned. I have no more dealings with you. If you have something to say, you'll have to take it up with my heavenly Father." In effect you will close the door at the end of each day, and not dwell on the past. Ralph Waldo Emerson stated it well: "Finish each day and be done with it. You have done what you could. Some blunders and absurdities no doubt crept in; forget them as soon as you can. Tomorrow is a new day; begin it well and serenely and with too high a spirit to be cumbered with your old nonsense."

4. MAKE THE CHANGES NECESSARY IN YOUR LIFE

The next step is to make the changes necessary in your life. It follows the third step as naturally as the rainbow follows the rain. The Psalmist explains it: "When my heart is right, then you will rejoice in the good that I do."

You need to change the thoughts, conversations, and deeds which lead you to feelings of guilt, to change your pattern of behavior. For example, a little boy snitched a quarter from his mother's purse. He felt guilty because he *was* guilty, but what did he need to do? Change his behavior. Instead of resorting to stealing, he needed to gain the money by earning it. In that way, the situation that created guilt feelings was resolved because he stopped stealing.

Perhaps you think, "But I want to do thus and so, even though it is wrong and even though it causes guilt within me." Let me remind you that if you check or change the expression of a desire, you will change the desire itself. By acting in a certain manner, you will eventually bring desire to coincide with your action.

5. MAKE RESTITUTION AS WISELY AND AS BEST YOU CAN

The final step is to make restitution as wisely and as best as you can. Restitution means to restore the good and right and to give an equivalent for loss or damage. It takes a well-directed, purposeful person with great courage to do it, but the results are worth it. An incident in the life of J. P. Bosovich, manager of a men's store in Grand Rapids, Michigan, illustrates the result.

Mr. Bosovich expressed surprise when he opened a letter containing a twenty dollar check and a note explaining that the money was from a woman who had stolen two sweaters from his store. The woman signed her name and gave her address in Ohio. She volunteered to send more if the twenty dollars wasn't enough. "Nothing like this has ever happened to me during all my years as a clothier," Bosovich exclaimed. The woman closed her letter by saying that she had turned her life over to God and this was one of the things she felt she must do to live out her new faith. Such restitution effectively handles guilt feelings.

I have used two key words in reference to resolving guilt feelings. They are "accept" and "apply." When principles for relieving guilt feelings are not consciously accepted and applied, a gnawing guilt dominates.

My family spent a Fourth of July with a couple who are members of the church I pastor. Their hideaway is on a lake, so, naturally, I had to try my hand at fishing. The fish were biting, but they were not swallowing the hook. Every time I pulled in my line, there was only a tidbit of bait left. The fish had nibbled it to death.

When guilt is not properly dealt with, it can nibble to death your vitality and effectiveness.

Christian meditation conditions you to experience the presence of God in such a way that you are eager to accept and apply the principles for releasing guilt feelings.

IN REVIEW

Accept responsibility for guilt feelings.
Avoid taking on the guilt feelings of others.
Bring guilt feelings to God.
Make the changes necessary in your life.
Make restitution as wisely and as best you can.

Dealing with Tension

6

Read the Scriptures slowly and meditatively

Let the peace of Christ rule in your hearts, remembering that as members of the one body you are called to live in harmony, and never forget to be thankful for what God has done for you.

Let Christ's teaching live in your hearts, making you rich in true wisdom. Teach and help one another along the right road....

Whatever work you may have to do, do everything in the name of the Lord Jesus, thanking God the Father through him.

(Col. 3:15-17, Phillips)

I am fascinated by a poster which shows a gigantic, single-edged razor blade. A man is tiptoeing barefoot on the blade, juggling in one hand a house overflowing with furnishings, and in the other, cars, boat, etc. The name of the blade is "Tension."

We are living in tense times. One man I heard of went in for a physical examination. After the checkup, the doctor said, "Your nerves are bad. I wouldn't be surprised if you drink twelve to fifteen cups of coffee a day." Trembling, the man answered, "Doc, I spill that many!"

I have heard that tension is the price of progress, but I do not honestly believe that God designed the human body and emotional system to undergo the conditions we have created for ourselves.

Let's examine the word tension. It originates from a Latin word which means "to stretch." It implies that an object is strained until it is pulled apart. I know an executive who was so tense in the back and shoulders that he could not turn his neck either to the right or left. But tension is first in the mind; that is, tension is a mental strain and tautness. It is both rooted in and accompanied by anxiety. The sufferer often experiences little nervous twitches in one place or another and muscles tighten up.

There are several noteworthy tension bombs in our day.

1. FANATICAL STRIVING

One is fanatical striving, overly tense effort. You feel like the deep-sea diver who was on the ocean floor investigating an old wrecked ship. Above was the mother ship to which his air hose was connected. Over the intercom connected to his suit, he heard this terrifying news. "Come up at once! The ship is sinking!"

2. OVERREACTION TO DEMANDS

Another bomb is overreaction to demands; for example, to requirements of the boss, the job, the family, and the society.

"The boss pushes me too hard," you feel.

"The job is too much for me."

"The family is too demanding."

In answer to the question, "Which are the best ten years of life?" someone replied, "My best ten years were eight to eighteen. Then I got married." One young man whose wedding was only weeks away browsed through a bookstore. He picked up *Man Against Himself,* flipped a few pages, then put it down. He picked up *The Art of Loving,* looked it over, and put it back on the shelf. Finally, he selected *How to Live with a Neurotic.*

One eighty-year-old, spirited woman insisted, "My best years are *now!* I refuse to live in the past. There's nothing there. It's all ahead. Life can be beautiful if we let it."

3. JUMPING TO CONCLUSIONS

Another tension bomb is the habit of jumping to conclusions. This humorous story of a man and his wife illustrates the point.

When the wife suddenly became critically ill, her husband rushed her to the emergency room. Soon the doctor came out and asked him for a chisel. He wondered about the reason, but found one anyway. Then the doctor came out of the emergency room and asked him for a hammer. His curiosity increased enormously, yet he found a hammer. Finally the doctor came and asked him for a hacksaw. "Look," asked the nervous husband, "just what are you doing to my wife?" The doctor replied, "Nothing. I am just trying to get my satchel open."

Situations which a person supposes to be true can cause tension even if he is wrong and has jumped to a conclusion. He thinks something is true and he responds as though it were true.

4. THE PACE OF LIFE

The fourth tension bomb is the unnatural pace of life in our industrialized society. It is that "hurry-worry-bury" routine we can all so easily fall into. It is senseless, and damaging, to let this pace destroy our lives. It is a "tempest in a teapot." Eventually the steam begins to rise out of the spout and there is a boil-over.

However, the total elimination of tension is not the answer. As I mentioned in my book *Discoveries for Peaceful Living,* the person who has no room for tension has no room for adventurous and successful living. You will never be the person you can be if all the pressure, tension, and discipline are taken out of your life. What we need is *control.* Here the Bible provides some answers.

1. "ALTITUDE" OF SOUL

Altitude of soul means to have inner assurance of the "peace that Christ gives" and to know that "to this peace God has called you" (Col. 3:15, TEV). What is the soul?

Man has never really been able to make a comprehensive analysis of the soul, but this we do know: The soul is to our spiritual nature what the heart is to the body. As a matter of fact, the soul is often referred to as "heart" in the Scripture. The heart is absolutely essential to the flow of blood in the body. The soul is the focus of your capacity to love, and know, and experience God. It is the peace-center of your life. Perhaps I can illustrate this by relating the story about Ben Franklin I read in *Guideposts Magazine.**

This was not the original Ben Franklin. Yet he had some qualities like his namesake. He was born on the plains of Kansas and, as a boy, Ben went camping in the mountains of Colorado. He was utterly fascinated by the ridges, the rugged rock, and the grandiose, snow-topped Rockies stretching into the beautiful blue skies.

At nine years of age, he was hiking up long trails and conquering tough summits. He felt free sleeping under the stars and listening to the wind blowing through the towering pines. The smell of the mountains and the singing streams tumbling from the heights brought music to his soul.

Ben Franklin became addicted to the mountains. He loved them and he thought that they loved him. He was a part of them and, most assuredly, they were a part of him. During the school year back in Kansas, he daydreamed of the trails and rock formations. Ben really started to live when school ended and he could rush to the mighty challenges of the slopes.

One day, when he was eighteen years of age, Ben was climbing with two friends when his rope was cut on a jagged edge. It broke and sent him hurtling 150 feet below. As a result of the fall, his back was broken in four places and his pelvis in two. But he was still alive. One friend stayed with Ben while the other ran for help. Everything seemed dark to Ben, and he wondered why the mountains had turned against him. By the time a rescue squad arrived, he was delirious. They strapped him tightly to a stretcher and rushed him to the hospital in Denver some thirty miles away. There surgeons worked

*From "What the Mountain Did to Me," copyright January 1972 by Guideposts Associates, Inc. Used by permission of GUIDEPOSTS MAGAZINE.

feverishly to save Ben's life, and they succeeded; but he was paralyzed from the waist down.

After a long stay in intensive care, Ben was told by his doctor, "Ben, you're a man and I've got to give it to you straight. You'll never walk again. You'll have to use a wheelchair." Ben thought about his legs. Once they were like powerful pistons propelling him up the mountains. Now they would be useless. Ben struggled to accept his condition as the days dragged on. Hospital orderlies turned over, washed, and dressed the embittered and rebellious young man.

After six months of helplessness, Ben blurted out, "OK, God. I surrender to you. I put myself in your hands. You know, Lord, that I don't want to be this way. If you choose not to give me full use of my legs, then give me full use of myself."

Soon a deep peace invaded Ben's heart, to an extent he had never experienced before, not even in the mountains. Somehow, deep down, he believed that he would have full use of himself, even if his legs remained still.

The next night, he moved a toe. Ben could hardly believe it! In his excitement, he shouted for the nurse. Crying, Ben said, "Look! My toe!" and he wiggled it.

Exuberantly, Ben leaned over and tried to kiss her. She ran from the room to call the doctor! With tears streaming down his face, Ben said, "Thank you, Lord. I'm gonna get full use of myself."

Today Ben uses heavy braces, but the wheelchair is gone. In fact, he put it aside after just a year. The young man went on to college and graduated with honors from the University of Colorado, where he was one of thirty students out of 15,000 named to "Who's Who in American Universities and Colleges."

That young man began to experience peace in the spiritual activity center known as his soul. He was able to take command of the tensions which confronted him. It is not unlikely that Ben might still be a victim of tension and confined to uselessness had he not discovered the peace of God in his soul.

There are little storms raging inside every one of us and they threaten to sweep us away. Tension can build up and force us out of control. We need to call in the master of wind and wave whose peace gives altitude of soul. Low-flying souls are bumped and dumped by the knocks of life, for without the "peace that Christ gives ... and to which God has called you" it is easy to succumb to conditions. After going to pieces, you have to pick up the pieces, if life is going to be life instead of a left-over.

How do you get this peace that gives altitude of soul? Not by grabbing or demanding. Rather by giving yourself, as you are and where you are. It is by acceptance of the peace which Christ gives and to which God calls you.

2. GRATITUDE OF MIND

In addition, control of tension requires gratitude of mind. "And be thankful" (Col. 3:15, TEV).

Gratitude is that thankful spirit which can produce remarkable results. It brightens up and enriches your attitude. Schopenhauer, the German philosopher, claimed that to one man, life is barren, dull, and superficial; whereas to another, life is interesting and full of meaning. The difference is within the man; attitude is more important than aptitude. In fact, aptitude can be changed and redirected by attitude. Philosopher William James stated that the greatest discovery of his generation was that human beings could change their lives by altering their attitudes. That is still true. Let me illustrate by sharing a story about a man of ordinary means.

The tax assessor came to reassess the value of the man's property. "I am a rich man," the gentleman beamed. Looking around, the assessor saw very common things. "Well, he's got a lot more than what meets the eye," he thought. "Tell me about it," the assessor said as he sharpened his pencil and grinned. The man replied, "I have a wife who understands and accepts me. And I have healthy, growing, and sometimes mischievous children. They're worth more than money can buy. Then I have something to do with my life that really counts. What a treasure that is! I also have a merry heart which enables me to meet life joyfully, and tough challenges which hone me down, and sharpen me up, and push me ahead. I have God as my partner. He gives focus to my life, enlightens the way, and goes with me everywhere." The official answered, "You are a rich man, and the property you've mentioned is not subject to taxation."

True gratitude destroys fault-finding and eliminates grumbling. It gently leads your faith to new levels. One of the most wonderful results of gratitude is that it enlarges your capacity to receive blessings. Sincere appreciation for little blessings prepares the way for bigger blessings, and stretches your spirit to accept and absorb them.

Gratitude reinforces your courage so that you can win over or get through any circumstance which life throws at you. The reason, simply, is that gratitude grows fortitude.

Dietrich Bonhoeffer, the German Christian who was killed by the Nazi regime, accurately stated it when he said that evil always carries the seeds of its own destruction. In *Letters and Papers from Prison*, he wrote, "I believe that God can and will give us all the strength we need to help us resist in all times of distress, but he never gives it in advance."

Gratitude of mind anticipates a good outcome no matter how long it takes for the good to come. Good does not always come quickly, but since we are the impatient generation, we want everything now, if not sooner. Gratitude of mind causes you to think, believe, hope, and work for a good outcome, and to hang on until the good appears. Eventually, you witness to good in reality. Such a spirit of gratitude keeps current events and conditions in spiritual perspective; thus, tension-makers become controlled by a tension breaker.

Specifically, what can you do to grow gratitude of mind? These six suggestions have been of great value to me.

1. Upon awakening, use a spiritual starter for the day. Some examples are: Psalm 118:24: "This is the day which the Lord hath made. We will rejoice and be glad in it." Romans 8:37: "We are more than conquerors through him who loved us" (RSV). The Doxology is very good: "Praise God from whom all blessings flow; praise him all creatures here below. Praise him

above, ye heavenly hosts; praise Father, Son, and Holy Ghost." If you use a spiritual starter during the first one or two minutes after you wake up, your mind and life will be pointed in the direction of a grateful day.

2. Tell God often that you are thankful. It is important to be definite, for that reminds you of the reality of your gratitude.

3. Remember the "little blessings," too. Many little ones become equivalent to a big one, and many small blessings strewn throughout the day cover the whole day with blessings.

4. Keep your mind on what you have. In that way, you will find that you probably have more than you thought and you will get more out of what you have.

5. Express gratefulness to other people often. Don't be surprised when you and they are blessed. Most assuredly, you will become a person they want as a friend.

6. Spend a couple of minutes in praise and prayer before you retire for the night, as a beautiful, "Good-night, God."

Through gratitude, I believe that you will discover the truth of what Sister Louise and the Sisters of the Cross said to me on an original card sent from Grand Rapids, Michigan.

> The joy of enjoying
> And the fullness of living
> Are found in the heart
> That is full of thanksgiving.

3. SERVITUDE OF LIFE

The third step in tension control is servitude of life. "Everything you do ... should be done in the name of the Lord Jesus" (Col. 3:17, TEV).

A store in Jackson, Mississippi, wisely displays this motto: "Service is the rent we pay for the space we occupy." As Archbishop Nathan Soderblom used to say, "Doctrine divides, but service unites." Dr. Peter Marshall conveyed the same idea when he told his great congregation in Washington, D.C., that the measure of life is not its duration, but its donation.

Charles Brown of Yale got across the point in an address to students at the University of California. He stated, "I come from a larger university than this. It is larger than Columbia, Yale, or all the American universities combined. It is the University of Life. Our colors are black and blue, for we learn from our lessons by hard knocks. In this university there is only one examination day, and in that examination there is but one question. It is that question that I have come to ask you. What is life?" Dr. Brown continued, "Let's ask the Great Teacher of all the ages, and hear his answer by word and deed: Life is service, for 'even as the Son of man came not to be ministered unto, but to minister....' "

Servitude, rightly understood, is a crucial concept: It is what you do with your life during the time God gives you. Then the question to be faced is, "What are you doing, for whom, and for what?" In my own experience, I always try to keep the following creed in mind: God in my life today; God through my life today, wherever I am, whatever I'm doing.

Every believer can be involved in "full-time Christian service." That includes the doctor, teacher, engineer, secretary, housewife, mechanic, executive, salesman, student, and teen-ager. And you do not have to change your vocation and become a church professional such as an ordained minister or a missionary. The only criterion is doing with your life, during the time God gives you, that which God wills for you. It means acting in the spirit of Jesus toward those who need your services.

A man by the name of Carter wanted Tony Ruloff, a painter, to redo the inside of an old mansion which he had bought.* As Tony looked over the place, he knew it would be a big job. "You won't be able to make a new house out of it," Tony said, "but this paint job is going to bring you pleasure or you won't owe me a cent." Carter appeared rather surprised until Tony explained the philosophy he and his wife have about business.

Even a humble business such as house painting, he stated, can be God's business if we want it to be. The test of whether God is in it is whether the transaction works for the highest good of every person involved.

On the following Monday morning, Tony and two of his five employees began the work. After two weeks, Carter said, "Ruloff, you're doing a sloppy job," and he proceeded to point out nicks which were almost invisible in the woodwork. Tony replied, "We want everyone to feel right about this job." After that, Carter followed the painters around like an old hen looking over her chicks. Continually he peered over their shoulders, delivering a barrage of comments and instructions about painting, although he had never picked up a brush in his life. On Friday, both of Tony's employees said that they wouldn't be back the next week. Tony assured them, "I have another job you can go to, but somehow or other I'm going to satisfy Mr. Carter." "Ha," they scoffed, "that's humanly impossible."

Tony transferred two more of his painters to the job. "I want you to paint better than you know how," he instructed them. "Not for Mr. Carter, and not for me, but for God." The work they were doing was more like refinishing than painting. When Tony checked with Carter to see if he was willing to pay the extra money required, Carter said, "Yes." A job which normally would have taken two weeks stretched into two months. When Carter got the final bill, he paid only three-fourths of it, saying he didn't remember any verbal agreement. The check wasn't enough to pay Tony's expenses.

After further conversation with Carter, Tony said, "OK. If you are sure your payment is right with God, I'll close the book on your deal." Carter indicated that he was sure. When Tony lost money on that job, a friend told him, "You're a bad businessman." But in Tony's own words, "I believe that God will never leave those who are doers of the Word shortchanged. God's law is 'Give and it shall be given unto you. Full measure, pressed down and running over shall it be given unto you.' I accepted Mr. Carter's payment and also his explanation that he couldn't remember what our final deal was. Carter and I are on good terms today. He will invite me in for coffee and I can feel him swell with pride as he looks around his house. As to my financial loss, I can only say that in the years since I painted Mr. Carter's house, business has never been so good. I have more work today than I can handle."

Servitude, as taught by Jesus, requires creative use of our time. It includes others. Therefore, rather than wasting time, energy, and thought on tension producers, we must learn to invest time, energy, and thought in service.

IN REVIEW

Remember the picture I mentioned at the beginning of this chapter? The razor blade poster was entitled: "Tension." It was a picture of life without faith. We have seen how to combat tension through:

ALTITUDE OF SOUL
GRATITUDE OF MIND
SERVITUDE OF LIFE

All three are served well by Christian meditation, which daily increases your awareness of God. He enables you to deal with feelings, demands, and circumstances which can cause tension.

Taming Your Temper

Read this passage slowly and meditatively

But now, put all these things behind you. No more evil temper or furious rage: no more evil thoughts or words about others, no more evil thoughts or words about God, and no more filthy conversation.

As, therefore, God's picked representatives of the new humanity, purified and beloved of God himself, be merciful in action, kindly in heart, humble in mind.

Accept life, and be most patient and tolerant with one another, always ready to forgive if you have a difference with anyone. Forgive as freely as the Lord has forgiven you.

(Col. 3:8, 12, 13, Phillips)

Uncontrolled temper is one of man's worst enemies, for it can make life impossible, almost unlivable.

A story is told about Jonathan Edwards, the third president of Princeton University and a great preacher and thinker. He had a daughter who had an uncontrolled temper. But her rages were unknown to all except members of the family.

A young man fell in love with her and wanted to marry her. When he asked permission, Dr. Edwards said sharply, "You can't have her." "But I love her," answered the young man. "You still can't have her," Dr. Edwards insisted. "Why?" the young man asked. Dr. Edwards answered, "Because she is not worthy of you." The young man persisted, "But she's a Christian, isn't she?" "Yes," answered Dr. Edwards, "she's a Christian, but the grace of God can live with some people with whom no one else can."

An uncontrolled temper is an indication of a deeper problem. It can be the sign of an inferiority complex. Sometimes a person resorts to emotional outbursts, thinking that they will compensate for his feelings of inadequacy and inability to communicate effectively.

Imbalanced people often lose their tempers. The less common sense a person demonstrates, the more apt he is to lose his temper. This reaction indicates that his mind is not trained to accept failures and disappointments, and he finds it easier to lose his temper than to face reality.

Uncontrolled temper is an irrational confrontation with disappointment. Toscanini, the famous maestro, was well known for his ferocious temper. When members of his symphony played poorly, he would pick up anything in sight and dash it to the floor. During one rehearsal, the tuba player hit an incredibly flat note. Toscanini grabbed his priceless watch and hurled it against the nearest wall, breaking it into a dozen pieces.

At the next rehearsal, his devoted orchestra members presented him with a luxurious, velvet-lined box containing two watches. One was a matchless timepiece and the other was a cheap, dime-store variety on which was inscribed: For Rehearsals Only.

Many of us confront disappointment in an irrational manner because sometimes it seems easier to be controlled by temper than to control it.

The capacity for temper is a valuable asset, for it is that capacity which can be the driving force behind our actions. Our capacity to act strongly and enthusiastically is the steam in the boiler that makes the wheels go round. The more vigorous that capacity, the more potentially useful a person is. The apostle Peter is a good example of this.

Known as the fiery disciple, Peter once vehemently denied any knowledge and association with Jesus. Yet he was the one to step on the water in an attempt to meet Christ. He had the capacity to act with enthusiasm. When this power was divinely harnessed, he became the leader of the early Christians. We see him filled with God's Holy Spirit on the Day of Pentecost, declaring to those before whom he had previously cowed, that Jesus is the Christ. Later, we see Peter as an instrument of God's healing power, as he ministers to a man crippled since child-hood. Although Peter was a man of ordinary education, he wrote two books contained in the best-seller of all time—the Bible.

TEMPER IS AN EMOTION

Once I defined "emotion" as a state of the mind reflected in the body by a response, either good or bad. This is illustrated by the person who sat nervously waiting for me to come back to my office so that she could give me a "piece of her mind." At the time, she was really "going to pieces." I invited her into my office. When she sat down, I noticed that her hands were shaking and her face was red and flushed. Her mouth and jaws quivered. Then she began to express "a piece of her mind." The woman (who did depart somewhat less troubled) was in an emotionally insecure frame of mind, and it made her quite ineffective. Mentally, physically, and spiritually, she was out of shape for the contest; the body reacted to it by developing a chemical disorder. She was overheated with anger.

That was also the case with a man who had been trying to phone his home for over an hour, but kept getting a busy signal. Finally, he asked the operator if she would cut in on the line. "Only if it's a matter of life and death, sir," she replied. "Well, I can tell you this," declared the man. "If that's my teen-age daughter on the line again, there's going to be a killing!"

Anger can produce a physical reaction in your nervous system. A physician told me, "Emotionally tight muscles produce pain in the back of the neck, in the stomach, in the colon, in the scalp, in blood vessels, in skeletal muscles. Emotionally tight muscles produce ulcer-like pains, gall bladder-like pains, common headaches, and migraine headaches." Dr. John Schindler in his book, *How to Live 365 Days a Year*, wrote that "emotional stress can be greater than any other stress; emotions usually act for a longer time than do other stressors, and they can produce the same effects as any other type of stress."

Anger affects breathing. Fired-up emotions increase your rate of breathing, which in turn can cause hyperventilation. The carbon dioxide level gradually drops until abnormal things of all sorts start happening. One man hyperventilated in the dentist's chair. All day he dreaded the visit to the dentist. He finally fell apart when he sat down in the chair and looked at all the contraptions surrounding him and realized they were about to be used in his mouth. He went into a state of mini-convulsions.

Anger has a direct bearing on your health. Dr. Alexis Carrel, the brilliant French physician and Nobel Prize winner, once stated that "emotions induce striking modifications of the bodily tissues." Another physician said that "good emotions are the greatest power for your good health that we know anything about."

Dr. Paul White, the famous heart specialist, illustrated this truth in *The Annals of Internal Medicine.* A surgeon performed a lengthy operation on a man to remove a cancer. A few days after the surgery, the doctor said that the patient was going to die. Medically, he was safe in making the prognosis, but he failed to take into account Henry's optimism and will to live. "Henry," another doctor asked as he entered the hospital room, "how are you today?" The patient was barely conscious, yet he managed a smile and determinedly replied, "OK, Doc. And I'm going to be out of here in a few days." Henry's attitude remained cheerful and determined, and he recovered. "So what?" someone asks. "He would have anyway." But the team of physicians attending Henry agreed that "if he had accepted the emotions of despair and defeat that his condition warranted, we are sure Henry would have died."

The scientific explanation for Henry is that the good emotions (will, determination, and cheer) produced a maximum hormone balance in his body, making up for what medicine alone could not do. I add this spiritual observation: Those good emotions in Henry were God's healing power and love at work in his mind and body. Dr. William R. Parker, the psychologist and author of *Prayer Can Change Your Life,* accurately described the phenomenon by saying, "What the deep mind desires, apparently the body will cooperate to do."

TEMPER IS THE WRONG USE OF ENERGY

The effect of temper on the body illustrates the wrong use of energy. Do not think that you tame temper by destroying the capacity for temper. Instead, you tame it by controlling it. Temper is controllable if you *want* to control it. How can that control be achieved? Here is a principle which needs to be indelibly written in your heart.

*YOU TAME TEMPER BY
REDEMPTION,
REPLACEMENT,
AND REDIRECTION
OF SPIRITUAL AND EMOTIONAL
ENERGY*

Review Colossians 3:8, 12, 13, quoted at the beginning of this chapter, to find out how to redeem, replace, and redirect emotional and spiritual energy.

1. POUR-OUT PROCESS

First, there is the pour-out process. "Now, put all these things behind you. No more evil temper or furious rage...."

To get a picture of this process, imagine that you hold in your hand a glass full of water. It is stagnant water, greenish in color and covered with a sickening scum. Naturally, it has a repelling odor. Now imagine that you pour out that stagnant water. Have you taken away the capacity of the glass to contain water? No. You have simply poured out the undesirable, making it possible to fill the glass with clean, cool, fresh water. That's the pour-out process.

I remember a man who had the nastiest temper one can imagine. It had gotten him into more trouble than I have space to discuss; for example, one day he flew into a rage and his boss fired him. On the way home, he stopped by his pastor's office and said, "I'll never lose my temper again."

The evening after that pledge, his seventeen-year-old son did something that teed him off. The man picked up the phone and called his pastor. "Reverend," he said, "I'm going to die if I don't blow my stack." The minister answered, "Go ahead and die. God bless you." Having said that, the minister hung up the phone and went about his work.

The next day, the man came to see the minister. He had a new look, a new confidence, and a new radiance as he said, "I died last night." He was talking about the loss of his uncontrollable temper. He had poured it out.

One great and universal wish of humankind expressed in religions, art, philosophy, and human life itself is the wish to transcend self. Through Jesus Christ, you can do it. In the case of temper, it involves the pour-out process—surrendering the emotion and personality into God's hands.

2. POUR-IN PROCESS

Next is the pour-in process. "Put on then, as God's chosen ones ... compassion, kindness, lowliness" (Col. 3:12, RSV). Let's go back to the picture of stagnant water. It has been poured out of the glass; therefore, the glass is empty, but it has the capacity to be filled with something else.

In the world of the spiritual, something must occupy that space. That is, it will not remain empty. Therefore, pour in life-building qualities such as compassion, kindness, and humility. They will make use of the energy and thoughts once diverted to uncontrolled temper. A man who can tell you that this works in an amazing manner is Ed—one of the most ill-tempered human beings you can imagine. Let me add that Ed is one of the largest men I've met: 6'7" and 250 pounds.

As Ed told me, he lived under the guilt of past mistakes, failures, and defeats. "I let them give me a defeatist frame of mind," he confessed. "They sort of hung over me like a sinister cloud about to unleash its stormy fury." To these facts in his life, Ed responded with anger. "I blamed God, other people, and circumstances," he stated.

One day Ed came across some verses in the Bible similar to the ones we are considering in this chapter. Reading the Bible was a new experience for him. He had started the practice on the advice of a business associate. "Like a bolt out of the clear," Ed explained, "it occurred to me that if I let God fill me, I could overcome my anger, get rid of guilt feelings, gain a new attitude, and live up to my potential." When Ed mentioned this to a Christian friend, he was told that he could begin by accepting Jesus Christ into his life. "That threw me," Ed said. "What is 'accepting Christ?' I asked."

His friend explained that "accepting Christ" means to humbly acknowledge your need for the Lord, turn your life over to him, receive his Spirit into your heart and mind, and begin living Christ's way. Ed seemed surprised that it wasn't more fanatical. Instantly, he recognized it to be the correct way to commit his life to God. Ed enthusiastically, yet quietly, responded. "Christianity became personal," he smiled, "meaningful, great! And, miraculously, I have begun to master my anger."

It is true that the mind does not stay empty for long. To enjoy the victory of pouring in, fill your mind with thoughts about Christ. Choose incidents from the Gospels that show his love, control, calmness, and concern. Recount, or look up, some promises of peace and power.

My Granny Ray was a remarkable woman. She stood about five feet tall, was lightweight, and a redhead, as were most of the Lucases in Hill County, Texas, from whence she came. And she had an enormous capacity for temper.

When pushed to wit's end, she would use Bible verses to redeem, replace, and redirect her spiritual and emotional energy. Through thoughts on Christ, she found that she could resist the temptation to give in to temper. You can, too!

3. POUR-ON PROCESS

The third step is the pour-on process. "Accept life, and be most patient and tolerant with one another, always ready to forgive if you have a difference with anyone" (Col. 3:13, Phillips).

You have poured out angry thoughts.

You have poured in Christlike thoughts.

Now you put those Christlike thoughts into positive action by pouring them on others. Start with those near you and dear to you, such as your wife, husband, children, father, mother, brother, sister, and fellow workers.

Dr. Thomas P. Malone of Atlanta, Georgia, has said, "In my practice, people sometimes ask me what psychiatry is all about. To me, the answer is increasingly clear. Almost every emotional problem can be summed up in one particular bit of behavior; it's a person walking around screaming, 'For God's sake, love me.' Love me, that's all. He goes through a million different manipulations to get somebody to love him.

"On the other hand, healthy people are those who walk around looking for someone to love. And, if you see changes in the people who are screaming, 'Love me, love me,' it's when they realize that if they give up this screaming and go to the other business of loving another human, they get the love they've been screaming for all their lives. It's hard to learn, but it's good when you learn it."

FOREBEARANCE AND FORGIVENESS

This positive living toward others requires forebearance and forgiveness. Forebearance means to bear far; literally, to go far; to go the second and third mile in relationships with others, in spite of their responses. It is love in action. Forgiveness is to make allowances for the shortcomings of others. It, too, is love in action.

But, as a man said to me, forebearance and forgiveness are hard. Once a little boy grunted and sweated as he carried a large rock to the backyard. His father asked, "Why don't you use all your strength?" The boy felt hurt and replied, "Daddy, I am." His father answered, "You haven't asked me."

Have you asked God to help you tame your temper?

Have you turned your emotions, as well as your heart, over to Christ?

Have you committed your disposition to the Lord?

We commonly think of conversion in terms of morals. But we also need our emotions and disposition converted. Have you asked God to help you? Ask him.

Christian meditation makes you aware of the God who waits and is willing to help you.

IN REVIEW

Temper is an emotion which needs to be tamed.

Control of temper can be realized by redemption, replacement, and redirection of spiritual and emotional energy.

This is possible by surrendering self and your temper to God, filling your thoughts with Christ, and forebearing and forgiving others.

Overyoming Worry 8

Read this passage slowly and meditatively

No one can serve two masters; for either he will hate the one and love the other, or he will be devoted to the one and despise the other. You cannot serve God and mammon.

Therefore I tell you, do not be anxious about your life, what you shall eat or what you shall drink, nor about your body, what you shall put on. Is not life more than food, and the body more than clothing? Look at the birds of the air; they neither sow nor reap nor gather into barns, and yet your heavenly Father feeds them. Are you not of more value than they? And which of you by being anxious can add one cubit to his span of life? And why are you anxious about clothing? Consider the lilies of the field, how they grow; they neither toil nor spin; yet I tell you, even Solomon in all his glory was not arrayed like one of these. But if God so clothes the grass of the field, which today is alive and tomorrow is thrown into the oven, will he not much more clothe you, O men of little faith? Therefore do not be anxious, saying, 'What shall we eat?' or 'What shall we drink?' or, 'What shall we wear?' For the Gentiles seek all these things; and your heavenly Father knows that you need them all. But seek first his kingdom and his righteousness, and all these things shall be yours as well.

Therefore, do not be anxious about tomorrow, for tomorrow will be anxious for itself. Let the day's own trouble be sufficient for the day.

(Matt. 6:24-34, RSV)

Unfortunately, many people believe that worry is a necessity of modern life. At least, they act as though it is. Consequently, worry for them becomes as much a part of daily routine as going to work, reading the newspaper, or eating.

I am reminded of a dialogue by comic Jonathan Winters on NBC's weekend "Monitor" program a few years ago. In this sketch Winters became a professional worrier and put himself out for hire. A person could employ him to worry about anything or anyone. Parents called on Winters to worry for them about their teen-agers; young people hired him to take over their worries caused by "mean, stubborn, unsympathetic, backward-thinking" parents. Businessmen put all of their economic worries on Winters. The State Department unloaded worrisome nations on him and the President relaxed his mind from worrying about the hot spots around the world. Everyone else could be at ease and really live it up.

But after watching less than four minutes, we were at it again. We were worrying about the only one left to worry about— Jonathan Winters! We began to worry over whether he worried enough about *our* problems.

What are some sources of worry?

FEAR OF SITUATIONS AND CIRCUMSTANCES

One of the bases for worry is the fear of situations and demands. I had the pleasure of helping a woman in Texas who was sick with worry. When she woke up in the morning, she thought about her agenda for the day and she began to worry. She questioned, "Can I get it all done?" "Am I up to it?" "Am I able to do it right?" A sense of insecurity had overcome her.

FEAR OF TOMORROW

Another source of worry is the fear of tomorrow. This is a fear of the unseen, the unpredictable, and the unknown. When people have come to me with their worries, I have occasionally asked them to list specific reasons for their worry. In many cases, the reply has been, "I can't put my finger on any reasons." Former President Franklin D. Roosevelt spoke words of great wisdom about the fear of tomorrow. He said, "The only thing we have to fear is fear itself."

FEAR OF THE PAST

Another unsettling cause of worry is fear of the past. Events in a person's past can continue to haunt him in the present, disrupting his life. I remember the man who told me about his failures, "Yesterday speaks with greater force than today." The fears of yesterday haven't ended. They can still kick.

TO CHOKE

Consider the derivation of the word "worry." It comes from the Anglo-Saxon verb which means "to choke," and that is exactly what it does to you spiritually and mentally. Worry strangles your creativity and stifles your imagination. To some degree, it also affects you emotionally and physically.

A doctor with whom I am acquainted said he is convinced that countless thousands of people are ill from what he calls "dammed up anxiety." He commented, "They figure they've got to live with worry so they dam it up inside." He continued to say, "When anxiety can't find an outlet, it does the only thing it can do. It turns inward and infects the person's whole psychology and his physical condition as well. It renders him distinctly less than creative if not definitely ill."

Another doctor has said, "Worry affects the circulation, the heart, the glands, and the whole nervous system. It profoundly affects one's health."

A Johns Hopkins University doctor commented that worriers die sooner than nonworriers. When asked why, he replied, "We don't know exactly. But it's a fact! To live by worry means destruction of your body." A rhyme someone handed me gets to the point. "The people who live in worry invite death in a hurry."

Worry takes purpose out of life—purpose offered to you by the Spirit of Jesus Christ within you. An epitaph on an ancient

Roman tombstone describes a result of worry. It reads, "I was not. I was. I am not. I do not care." Loss of purpose is tragic. A purposeless person is like a drifting ship on a massive ocean, because he goes here and there under no power of his own.

My personal observation is that basically, worry is neither a psychological or physical problem. Instead, it is a spiritual problem, a spiritual cancer. As a result, it can have these effects on a person:

Worry minimizes faith. The worrier is too wrapped up in himself, things, and happenings to fully exercise his faith.

Worry inflates situations beyond their normal proportions. It makes a problem look much bigger than it really is. These lines by an unknown author describe it.

> Worry is an old man with bended head,
> Carrying a load of feathers
> Which he thinks is lead.

Worry hides the greatness of God. One who is wrought with worry has difficulty seeing how big and wonderful God is, and what he can do.

Worry buries the goodness of God. He is still good, but the worrier hides himself from that goodness. Worry puts up a barrier between him and his Creator.

Then it is imperative that you overcome worry or worry will overcome you. In the Sermon on the Mount, Christ outlined a reliable prescription for overcoming worry. It really works, as many Christians have discovered.

1. TICK-TICK LIVING

This masterful prescription includes "tick-tick living." That means that as a clock ticks a tick at a time, live your life a day at a time. "Don't worry at all then about tomorrow. Tomorrow can take care of itself!" (Matt. 6:34, Phillips). I recall a story I once heard which gets across this idea.

Once there was a grandfather clock that said, "I'm giving up. It's no use." A sofa nearby, which was wise to the ways of living, asked, "Why?" The clock answered, "Because I've just calculated that over the next 365 days I've got to tick 31,000,000 times, and I can't do all that." The practical-minded sofa replied, "You can tick a tick at a time. Now, it's this tick, not tomorrow's tick, that you need to worry about."

I wear a watch which is not as intelligent as that grandfather clock. Nevertheless, it isn't ticking a year at a time, or a month, or a week, or a day, or an hour. It is not even ticking a minute at a time. Rather, my watch is ticking only for this second.

Since living tomorrow today is one of life's biggest worry-producers, the Lord accurately pointed out that we are to live today *today*. However, Jesus never meant his words to be an excuse for a lack of preparation. He meant for them to provide relief from worry. Perhaps the farmer had the idea when he said that when he works, he works hard; when he sits, he sits loose; and when he worries, he falls asleep. We need to follow the advice of Mrs. Wiggs of the book *The Cabbage Patch,* who wisely stated that she makes it a practice to put all her worries in the bottom of her heart, sit on the lid, and smile.

God, who cares for you today, will care for you tomorrow—when tomorrow comes. He will either shield you or he will give you whatever you need to face the demands of that day. So be at peace within by putting aside your worry.

2. SUBORDINATION OF THINGS

The divine prescription includes subordination of things. Jesus spent most of this Bible passage dealing with our attitude toward and use of possessions, not because he was obsessed with money, but because we are money-obsessed people. The average person's percentage of worry over "things" is abnormally high; therefore, the Lord said, "No one can serve two masters ... You cannot serve God and mammon [money]" (Matt. 6:24, RSV).

I want to clarify some confusion among Christian people. Christ does *not* say that you cannot serve God and possess things. Nor does he say that if you possess God, or if you are possessed by God, you cannot possess things. He says you cannot *serve* God and things simultaneously, and that you cannot be *possessed* totally by God and by things at the same time.

You must be the master of things that money can buy: food, clothes, medicine, shelter, etc. Jesus makes clear that:

>   (1) *You are a manager of what you have and not the ultimate owner.*
>   (2) *All that is given to you, or that you earn, or that is passed on to you, is a trust from God.*
>   (3) *You must place your value in the most important things; get your perspective in order; set your priorities straight.*
>   (4) *Use for the honor of God that which God entrusts to you.*

YOUR RESPONSIBILITY IS THAT OF A MANAGER

You are the manager of your body, mind, time, abilities, environment, family, children, money, and assets. The Christian recognizes God as the Lord over all, yet he rejoices that God has made him the master of the natural creation.

When a person is truly willing to let go of everything he possesses, he gains power over those possessions. He is freed from the awesome power of things to creatively enjoy all things. It is demonstrated in this way:

ALL BELONGS TO GOD→ YOU BELONG TO GOD→ EVERYTHING BECOMES YOURS IN, FROM, AND THROUGH GOD.

What a release it was for me when I began to discover this fact for myself. And what a victory over worry.

A conversion of attitude toward possessions can combat worry. In the quest to overcome worry, you cannot disregard this matter of possessions, for the Lord is total Lord of total life, and life involves the use of things.

3. TRUST IN THE LORD

The workable prescription for overcoming worry is rooted in trust in the Lord. "Seek first his kingdom and his righteousness, and all these things shall be yours as well" (Matt. 6:33, RSV). J. B. Phillips used this headline on the Scripture passage: "Put your trust in God alone."

I have trusted people and occasionally I have been disappointed. I am sure that people have trusted me and occasionally they have been disappointed. That is because all of us are created and we are human beings. But when we trust in the Lord, we rely on one who never fails.

RELATIONSHIP AND ACTS

Trusting God is a powerful worry-breaker, in that a *relationship* and *acts* are involved. This truth was brought home to me in a new way when I visited my nephew, Ricky, in a Memphis hospital.

In 1973, Ricky was the distributor for a large milk company in McCamey, Texas. Early one Saturday evening, the manager of a large supermarket called for more milk. Ricky loaded several cases in the back of his pickup and started off on the lonely and desolate twenty-mile trip. On the way, he had an accident. As far as safety investigators can determine, he tried to avoid a deer which probably ran across the road. At any rate, highway patrolmen found Ricky the next morning about 100 yards off the seldom-traveled highway, sprawled beside the pickup. He had been thrown clear of the vehicle and he had a soft spot on the crown of his head. They noticed that he couldn't move.

Ricky was rushed to a hospital in Odessa, Texas, where an examination revealed that his spinal cord had snapped, probably from hitting his head violently against the inside top of the cab of his pickup. At age twenty-four, he was totally paralyzed from the shoulders down, and, at best, he could expect to be confined to a wheelchair for life.

For the next three years, Ricky couldn't have cared less whether he lived or died. Such despair and depression gripped him that he was like the man who thought he would have to die to feel better. In Memphis, he told me how he had made a career of doubt, self-pity, and hopeless outlook, in spite of the love, prayers, and encouragement of family and friends, and the large sums of money invested in his rehabilitation program.

However, something happened that began to change his life. It started when Ricky met a man who was in the very same physical condition as he. Ricky asked him how long he had been that way, and the man answered, "Twenty years." Ricky sighed, "I couldn't take twenty years in a wheelchair." The man replied, "I couldn't either if I didn't trust the Lord and believe that he wants to help me." Coming from one in the same predicament, these words reached Ricky as no one and nothing had for three years. The result is that his whole life began to change. Ricky began to trust in the Lord, and his relationship with this Christian man started him on a new course.

You ask, "How can I trust God in a way that affects my everyday life?" In reply, I submit these steps.

HOW TO TRUST GOD

First, open your life like it is and as much as you know how, to the Lord. This is a spiritual act of the heart and a conscious act of the mind. I have found out that an important part of conversion to Christ is *beginning*. It is a spiritual start.

I once knew a man who had little to do with church or Christianity, although he was an upstanding and moral individual. As a youngster, he had gone to Sunday school once in a while, and had attended a few worship services with his parents. In college he really took on life single-handedly. He developed a pattern that stayed with him until he was over forty years old, and at the pinnacle of his financial success. Then he felt that things don't offer everything a person needs. As we prayed together, he experienced a personal and honest activity with God. It was no proxy religion, no hand-me-down-religion, and no second-hand stuff. In his own way, he invited God to join him for life. I believe two things happened when he talked to God. One, he admitted the need as he knew it, and, two, he submitted himself, as he was, as much as he knew how, to Christ. That was possible because the man accepted the fact that

God loved him. That was a start.

First, you start.

Second, verbally thank God for accepting you. Do this in your own words.

Third, as soon as possible, speak a word or perform an act of trust to or for some other human being.

Fourth, keep opening your life to God a day at a time, at the beginning of each day. This brings us to the second side of spiritual conversion, which is the *continuation* of the Christian life you have begun.

A person said, "I don't think I'm a Christian." When I asked, "Why?" he said, "Well, I don't feel Christian. If I have any faith, it's no more than skin deep. I'm depressed a lot of the time. I don't seem to have any direction to my life now. I'm coasting. I don't have any get-up-and-go." After a few minutes of getting some facts, I told him that God does claim him as a redeemed child, but perhaps the problem is that after starting out as a child of God, he stopped.

The new life can be as fresh as the morning sun, but not on yesterday's commitment. Yesterday's faith had meaning to it, but you need to renew it for today. Living life in a spiritual past makes faith stale, stuffy, and eventually odorous. Dr. Samuel Shoemaker, in his book *Under New Management,* got across the point when he wrote "[The Christian life] is a continuous effort to live in Christ and for Him and by His help, seeking to strengthen and deepen our lives. Repeatedly, we fall far below that original commitment and decision, and have to be brought back to God for forgiveness and renewal." As the apostle Paul stated, "... be transformed by the renewal of your mind" (Rom. 12:2, RSV). In his book *The One and Only You,* Bruce Larson deals with this concept: "The idea of conversion which has been so frightening to many is nothing more than God offering us the possibility of change. It is a process of gaining rather than losing."

The Christian life is a *process,* too. And the process is energized by a daily renewal of your faith.

Fifth, in prayer, submit each need to the Lord when you

become aware of the need. A visible expression of submission has helped many people accept its reality. Cup your hands touching one another, opened upward. Picture the need in your cupped hands. Stretch out your hands from you as you pray, "Lord, this is the need as I see it. Now I am submitting it to you."

Scripture draws a very graphic picture of this process by using the word, "cast." "Cast all your anxieties on him [the Lord]" (1 Pet. 5:7, RSV).

It is like the man who told a friend that he hired someone to do all his worrying (much like the professional worrier). "You've got to be kidding," the friend answered in disbelief. "Somebody to do all your worrying for you?" He laughed. But he saw that the man was serious. He asked, "Well, how much do you have to pay the worrier?" The man replied, "$1,000 a week." Knowing that his friend was of average means, the friend exclaimed, "Where in the world are you going to get $1,000 a week?" The man calmly said, "That's his worry." That is what "cast" means. J. B. Phillips paraphrases the sentence, "You can throw the whole weight of your anxieties upon him [God]." The idea is to let go of them as you would a hot potato.

Sixth, feel free to question your faith. You may have thought that to question is to doubt, or that the person of faith does not and should not have an inquiring, seeking mind.

I remember a young couple who came to see me for an appointment. The woman, an attractive and thinking person, told me that she had more or less been a church dropout for several years. "The final blow," she stated, "was when I was instructed not to question the church; rather, to just accept it." To her, that meant blind discipleship.

I reminded her that questioning is *not* synonymous with doubt, and that doubt is not the same as an inquiring mind. Likewise, faith is not the companion of blind followership, and faith is not the same as empty obedience. Doubt is the refusal of the mind to accept, and of the life to act, when there is evidence that should be accepted and acted on.

Remember the Bible story of the Israelites on the border of the

Promised Land of Kadesh-barnea? The challenge before them was great. They faced a prosperous, well-organized, and finely equipped people. Moses recounted some of the times past when God had showed his power to deliver his people; for instance, when he freed them from bondage in Egypt. Moses then said: "The Lord God has given us this land. Go and possess it ... Don't be afraid! Don't even doubt!" (Deut. 1:21, TLB). The people sent twelve spies to look over the situation in Kadesh-barnea more closely. Those men returned with the report that "it was indeed a good land which the Lord our God had given us" (v. 25). Then we read the telltale liner of doubt: "But the people refused to go in ..." (vs. 26). Moses said, "Yet in spite of this word [the evidence] you did not believe the Lord your God" (v. 32, RSV).

We must test our faith by our willingness to act. To question your faith is to put it to a test, to strengthen it, and to enlarge its boundaries.

Seventh, make friends with people who encourage your faith to grow. Being part of a Christian group tangibly helps you win out over worry, for in and through the group you identify with other people of faith, hope, and love who also grapple with the realities of life.

Dr. E. Stanley Jones wrote in his book *Victorious Living:* "I am quite sure that I should not have survived as a Christian had I not had the corporate life of the Church to hold me up. When I rejoiced, they rejoiced with me. When I was weak, they strengthened me ... When I fell ... they gathered around me by prayer and love, and without blame or censure they lovingly lifted me back to my feet again."

The self-motivated, energetic, untiring, enthusiastic, and strong apostle Paul also needed such association. After writing, "I can do all things through Christ which strengtheneth me" (Phil. 4:13), he said of his friends, "But it was kind of you to share the burden of my troubles" (Phil. 4:14, NEB).

Eighth, each day acquaint yourself with a passage from the Bible, because it reinforces your trust in God. As you read, open your mind and life. Expect to be filled, and God's truth will transform your thoughts.

Ninth, keep believing that the future is really your friend. I think that Ralph Waldo Emerson expressed this thought well when he said, "What I have seen teaches me to trust the Creator for what I have not seen." Your future will be blessed by God because God is in your life today. What the future has in store for you depends largely on what you place in store for your future.

God desires for you to overcome worry. Trust him and you release his power to overcome, rather than to be overcome. Christian meditation increases your awareness of God to the extent that you are more willing to trust him with your whole life.

IN REVIEW

To overcome worry:
LIVE A DAY AT A TIME.
SUBORDINATE "THINGS."
TRUST IN THE LORD.

THE FINAL THOUGHT

He [God] gives power to the tired and worn out, and strength to the weak.

Even the youths shall be exhausted, and the young men will all give up.

But they that wait upon the Lord shall renew their strength. They shall mount up with wings like eagles; they shall run and not be weary; they shall walk and not faint.

(Isa. 40:29-31, TLB)

Resources

CHAPTER 1
I Came to It the Hard Way

Lane Adams, *How Come It's Taking Me So Long to Get Better?* (Wheaton, Illinois: Tyndale House Publishers, 1975).

CHAPTER 2
What Is Christian Meditation?

Charlie W. Shedd, *Getting Through to the Wonderful You* (Old Tappan, N.J.: Fleming H. Revell Company, 1976).

C. J. Jung, "The Psychology of Eastern Meditation," Collected Works, Vol. II *Psychology and Religion: East and West* (Princeton University Press, 1969).

CHAPTER 3
How Important Is Christian Meditation to You?

Hans Selye, *The Stress of Life* (New York: McGraw-Hill Book Company, 1956).

Paul Tournier, *The Meaning of Persons* (New York: Harper & Row, Publishers, 1957).

Dr. George C. Thosteson, "To Your Good Health," Jackson, Mississippi, *Daily News*, April 12, 1976.

Charles Colson, *Born Again* (Old Tappan, N.J.: Fleming H. Revell Company, 1976).

Alvin Toffler, *Future Shock* (New York: Random House, 1970).

Paul Tournier, *Learn to Grow Old* (New York: Harper and Row, Publishers, 1973).

Dale Moody, *Spirit of the Living God* (Nashville: Broadman Press, 1976).

J. Marmor, *Encyclopedia of Mental Health,* Vol. I (New York: Franklin Watts, Inc., 1963).

Gary R. Collins, *Overcoming Anxiety* (Wheaton, Illinois: Key Publishers, Inc., 1973).

Alfred M. Freedman, Harold J. Kaplan, and Benjamin J. Sadack, *Modern Synopsis of Psychiatry* (Baltimore: Williams & Wilkins Company, 1972).

CHAPTER 4
Basic Equipment and Grass Roots Elements of Christian Meditation

Herbert Benson, *The Relaxation Response* (New York: William Morrow Publishing Company, 1975).

CHAPTER 6
Dealing with Tension

David Ray, *Discoveries for Peaceful Living* (Old Tappan, N.J.: Fleming H. Revell Company, 1972).

Dietrich Bonhoeffer, *Letters and Papers from Prison* (New York: The Macmillan Company, 1962).

CHAPTER 7
Taming Your Temper

John Schindler, *How to Live 365 Days a Year* (Englewood Cliffs, N.J.: Prentice-Hall, 1954).

William R. Parker, *Prayer Can Change Your Life* (Englewood Cliffs, N.J.: Prentice-Hall, Inc., 1957).

CHAPTER 8
Overcoming Worry

Sam Shoemaker, *Under New Management* (Grand Rapids, Michigan: Zondervan Publishing House, 1966).

Bruce Larson, *The One and Only You* (Waco, Texas: Word Books, 1974).

E. Stanley Jones, *Victorious Living* (Nashville: Abingdon Press).

SEMINARS

"The Art of Christian Meditation" is also an eight-hour, non-denominational seminar which a growing number of people are discovering to be of enormous value in increasing their personal awareness of God.

The Christian Meditation Association, directed by a group of business men and women, is incorporated as a nonprofit organization to promote the practice of Christian meditation, using the techniques outlined in this book.

You may be interested in having a seminar in your church, business, community, or school. For complete information write:

> Mr. Allan G. Edgar
> Christian Meditation Association
> 1100 West Capitol Street
> Jackson, MS 39203

CHRISTIAN MEDITATION CASSETTE TAPE

One of the principles crucial to the success of Christian meditation is practice.

Not long ago, I saw the wife of a man who attended a seminar. When I asked about him, she replied, "For two months, he did great! His whole life took a sharp turn-around. But he stopped daily meditation and now he's in the same old defeated rut."

For a growing number of people, another vital element of success is the use of a guided meditation period until practice becomes second nature. To fill this need, we have prepared a Christian Meditation Cassette Tape.

On one side is a guided fifteen-minute meditation period in which you are led step by step in Christian meditation. On the reverse side is the body relaxation exercise.

Tapes may be ordered at $4.95 each from the address above.

ABILITY

Definition: Quality or state of being able; power to perform.

Meditation Verse: *"Be sure to use the ABILITIES God has given you ... Put these abilities to work; throw yourself into your tasks ..."* (1 Tim. 4:14, 15, TLB).

Explanation: **God has endowed you with abilities. Find and use them.**

ABOUND

Definition: To be in great quantity.

Meditation Verse: *"A faithful man will ABOUND with blessings"* (Prov. 28:20, RSV).

Explanation: **Overflowing blessings are promised to *you*.**

ABUNDANCE

Definition: An overflowing sufficiency.

Meditation Verse: *"God is able to provide you with every blessing in ABUNDANCE, so that you may always have enough of everything and may provide in ABUNDANCE for every good work"* (2 Cor. 9:8, RSV).

Explanation: **God will give you enough, and then some!**

ACTION

Definition: Something done or effected; behavior; conduct.

Meditation Verse: *"With the help of God we shall do mighty ACTS of valor"* (Psa. 108:13, TLB).

Explanation: **The sky is not your limit when God is on your side. He is!**

ANSWER

Definition: A reply; a correct reply.

Meditation Verse: *"Don't worry about anything; instead, pray about everything; tell God your needs and don't forget to thank him for his ANSWERS"* (Phil. 4:6, TLB).

Explanation: **God thinks enough of you to listen and reply.**

ASSURANCE

Definition: State of being assured, secure, certain.

Meditation Verse: *"Let us draw near [to God] with a true heart in full ASSURANCE of faith"* (Heb. 10:22, RSV).

Explanation: **Through your faith, you are assured of God's best.**

ATTITUDE

Definition: Posture (of the mind); indicates feeling or mood.

Meditation Verse: *"Let this MIND [attitude] be in you, which was also in Christ Jesus"* (Phil. 2:5).

Explanation: **If you have the mind of Christ, then you are prepared to mind his business, which is also to your benefit.**

BEAUTY

Definition: Having attractiveness or pleasurably exhalting the mind or spirit.

Meditation Verse: *"Your BEAUTY should not be dependent on an elaborate coiffure, or on the wearing of jewellery or fine clothes, but on the inner personality—the unfading loveliness of a calm and gentle spirit, a thing very precious in the eyes of God"* (1 Pet. 3:3, 4, Phillips).

Explanation: **The most beautiful creature is a person with a calm and gentle spirit.**

BEGIN

Definition: To do the first act; to take the first step; to start.

Meditation Verse: *"I feel sure that the one who has BEGUN his good work in you will go on developing it ..." (Phil. 1:6, Phillips).*

Explanation: **God, who has begun to work through your life, will not let you down.**

BELIEVE

Definition: To have faith or confidence; to think; to accept as true.

Meditation Verse: *"Whatever you ask in prayer, BELIEVE that you have received it, and you will" (Mark 11:24, RSV).*

Explanation: **Pray, and accept God's promises at face value.**

BELONG

Definition: To be connected with; to be attached to.

Meditation Verse: *"We each have different work to do. So we BELONG to each other, and each needs all the others" (Rom. 12:5, TLB).*

Explanation: **Life is a team experience. You belong to God's family. His family belongs to you.**

BOLDNESS

Definition: Quality of being unafraid to meet danger; confidence.

Meditation Verse: *"Be BOLD and strong! Banish fear and doubt! For remember, the Lord your God is with you wherever you go" (Josh. 1:9, TLB).*

Explanation: **God wants you to be a truly bold person.**

CALM

Definition: Freedom from agitation or disturbance.

Meditation Verse: *"He [God] CALMS the storm and stills the waves. What a blessing is that stillness"* (Psa. 107:29, 30, TLB).

Explanation: **You can become a calm person, even in a tempestuous world.**

CAN

Definition: To be able to do, make, or accomplish.

Meditation Verse: *"I CAN do all things through Christ which strengtheneth me"* (Phil. 4:13).

Explanation: **Everything God wants you to do, you can do!**

CARE

Definition: Charge of; management; a liking for.

Meditation Verse: *"I [God] have created you and* cared *for you since you were born. I will be your God through all your lifetime, yes, even when your hair is white with age. I made you and I will CARE for you. I will carry you along and be your Savior"* (Isa. 46:3, 4, TLB).

Explanation: **God does care for you deeply ... for as long as he lives—forever.**

CHANGE

Definition: To make different; to be altered.

Meditation Verse: *"Do not conform outwardly to the standards of this world, but let God transform you inwardly by a complete CHANGE of your mind. Then you will be able to know the will of God"* (Rom. 12:2, TEV).

Explanation: **The potential for positive change is your birthright as a child of God.**

CHEERFUL

Definition: A happy state of mind, spirit, feeling; gaiety.

Meditation Verse: *"When a man is gloomy, everything seems to go wrong; when he is CHEERFUL, everything seems right!" (Prov. 15:15, TLB). "Be of good CHEER, I have overcome the world" (John 16:33, RSV).*

Explanation: **You can be cheerful because God has overcome anything that could defeat you.**

CHOICE

Definition: Care in selection; power of choosing.

Meditation Verse: *"CHOOSE life ... CHOOSE to love the Lord your God and to obey him ... for he is your life and the length of your days" (Deut. 30:19, 20, TLB).*

Explanation: **Choice is one of the great freedoms you have. Choose God and life.**

CLOSE

Definition: Not far away.

Meditation Verse: *"The Lord is CLOSE to those whose hearts are breaking; he rescues those who are humbly sorry for their sins. The good man does not escape all troubles–he has them too. But the Lord helps him in each and every one" (Psa. 34:18, 19, TLB).*

Explanation: **Think of how the sunlight floods you on a bright day. God is closer to you than the sunlight.**

COMMIT

Definition: To give in trust; to consign.

Meditation Verse: *"COMMIT everything you do to the Lord. Trust him to help you do it and he will" (Psa. 37:5, TLB).*

Explanation: **Place your life and activity into God's hands. The odds for success are better that way.**

COMPLETE

Definition: Brought to an end; concluded.

Meditation Verse: *"Having started the ball rolling so enthusiastically, you should carry this project through to COMPLETION ..." (2 Cor. 8:11, TLB).*

Explanation: **Starting demands staying. God wants you to follow through to completion.**

CONCENTRATE

Definition: To direct toward or concentrate on a common center.

Meditation Verse: *"To SET the mind on the Spirit is life and peace" (Rom. 8:6, RSV).*

Explanation: **Take charge of your mind by setting it on God. Results: life and peace.**

CONFESS

Definition: To acknowledge; to make known.

Meditation Verse: *"If we CONFESS our sins, he is faithful and just, and will forgive our sins and cleanse us from all unrighteousness" (1 John 1:9, RSV).*

Explanation: **Acknowledge wrongdoing. God will forgive you.**

CONFIDENCE

Definition: State of feeling sure.

Meditation Verse: *"In returning and rest shall ye be saved; in quietness and in CONFIDENCE shall be your strength ..." (Isa. 30:15).*

Explanation: **God, rest, and quietness fill you with unbeatable confidence.**

CONTENT

Definition: Having desires limited to that which one has.

Meditation Verse: *"I have learned to be CONTENT, whatever the circumstances may be"* (Phil. 4:11, Phillips).

Explanation: **Restlessness is put to rest when you achieve the quality of contentment God offers.**

CONTROL

Definition: To keep within limits; to check or regulate.

Meditation Verse: *"A wise man CONTROLS his temper. He knows that anger causes mistakes"* (Prov. 14:29, TLB).

Explanation: **You can master your emotions by letting God master you.**

CONTROL

Definition: To keep within limits; to check or regulate.

Meditation Verse: *"God did not give us a spirit of timidity but a spirit of power and love and self-CONTROL"* (2 Tim. 1:2, RSV).

Explanation: **Self-control comes to you through God-control: God in control of you.**

COURAGE

Definition: That quality which enables one to meet danger and difficulties with firmness.

Meditation Verse: *"Don't be impatient. Wait for the Lord, and he will come and save you! Be brave, stout-hearted and COURAGEOUS. Yes, wait and he will help you"* (Psa. 27:14, TLB).

Explanation: **"Wait" means to invest the time to think upon. By waiting, God blesses you with an amazing sense of courage.**

CREATE (MAKE)

Definition: To bring into being; to cause to exist.

Meditation Verse: *"Day and night alike belong to you [God]; you MADE the starlight and the sun. All nature is within your hands; you MAKE the summer and the winter too" (Psa. 74:16, TLB).*

Explanation: **Your God is the one behind this universe. He also created you. You are important to him.**

DELIGHT

Definition: A high degree of gratification.

Meditation Verse: *"Take DELIGHT in the Lord, and he will give you the desires of your heart" (Psa. 37:4, RSV).*

Explanation: **God is great to get along with. You will discover a new vista of delight when you center your life in him.**

DILIGENCE

Definition: Perseverance; giving careful attention.

Meditation Verse: *"Giving all DILIGENCE, add to your faith virtue; and to virtue, knowledge; and to knowledge, temperance; and to temperance, patience; and to patience, godliness" (2 Pet. 1:5, 6, KJV).*

Explanation: **Diligence is a quality of spirit which opens the way to a full and clean life.**

DIRECTION

Definition: Guidance; management.

Meditation Verse: *"Show me the PATH where I should go, O Lord; point out the right ROAD for me to walk" (Psa. 25:4, TLB).*

Explanation: **God gives you the direction you desire. No more aimlessness or floating!**

ENCOURAGE

Definition: To inspire; to hearten, cheer on or up.

Meditation Verse: *"When I pray, you [God] answer me, and ENCOURAGE me by giving me the strength I need" (Psa. 138:3, TLB).*

Explanation: **God is the greatest encourager you have.**

ENCOURAGEMENT

Definition: Act of inspiring, cheering, heartening.

Meditation Verse: *"Anxious hearts are very heavy but a word of ENCOURAGEMENT does wonders!" (Prov. 12:25, TLB).*

Explanation: **When you encourage others, you are encouraged.**

ENDURE

Definition: State of capability of lasting; continuing.

Meditation Verse: *"Love bears all things, believes all things, hopes all things, ENDURES all things" (1 Cor. 13:7, RSV).*

Explanation: **You have what it takes to take it when you honestly love God.**

ENJOY

Definition: To have satisfaction, have the benefit of.

Meditation Verse: *"The Holy Spirit, God's gift, does not want you to be afraid of people, but to be wise and strong, and to love them, and ENJOY being with them" (2 Tim. 1:7, TLB).*

Explanation: **You are in this world to love God *and* enjoy him forever. He gives you a love for people, too.**

FAITH

Definition: Complete confidence; fidelity to one's promises.

Meditation Verse: *"None who have FAITH in God will ever be disgraced for trusting him" (Psa. 25:3, TLB).*

Explanation: **Faith is reliance on God. You are much better off when you depend on him.**

FAITHFULNESS

Definition: Firm in adherence to promises; true in affection or allegiance.

Meditation Verse: *"Every morning tell him [God], 'Thank you for your kindness,' and every evening rejoice in his FAITHFULNESS" (Psa. 92:2, TLB).*

Explanation: **Become a "keep-at-it" person. That's the secret of adventure in life.**

FAMILY

Definition: A group comprising immediate kindred; a group of closely related individuals.

Meditation Verse: *"I will try to walk a blameless path, but how I need your [God's] help, especially in my own home [FAMILY], where I long to act as I should" (Psa. 101:2, TLB).*

Explanation: **There are people who love you. Think of them as your family.**

FEELING

Definition: An emotional state; emotional responsiveness.

Meditation Verse: *"What awe we FEEL, kneeling here before him [God] ... The God of Israel gives strength and mighty power to his people. Blessed be God!" (Psa. 68:35, TLB).*

Explanation: **Your feelings are important, too. God gave you the capacity for feelings.**

FOREVER

Definition: A limitless time.

Meditation
Verse: *"For this great God is our God FOREVER and ever. He will be our guide until we die"* *(Psa. 48:14, TLB).*

Explanation: **Eternity is in you because God is forever and you are his child.**

FORGET

Definition: To cease remembering; to cease from doing.

Meditation
Verse: *"I am bringing all my energies to bear on this one thing: FORGETTING the past and looking forward to what lies ahead"* *(Phil. 3:13, TLB).*

Explanation: **Keep the past in the past. Let your concerns be for today.**

FORGIVE

Definition: To pardon.

Meditation
Verse: *"If my [God's] people who are called by my name humble themselves, and pray and seek my face, and turn from their wicked ways, then I will hear from heaven, and will FORGIVE their sin and heal their land"* *(2 Chron. 7:14, RSV).*

Explanation: **Forgiveness in God's eyes helps you to act as if you never sinned. He clears the record.**

FREEDOM

Definition: Liberation from imprisonment.

Meditation
Verse: *"The law of the Spirit of life in Christ Jesus has set me FREE..."* *(Rom. 8:2, RSV).*

Explanation: **God releases you to a new freedom of life in him.**

FRIENDSHIP

Definition: Attachment to another by esteem, respect, and affection.

Meditation Verse: *"But God is my helper. He is a FRIEND of mine" (Psa. 54:4, TLB).*
"Love forgets mistakes; nagging about them parts the best of FRIENDS" (Prov. 17:9, TLB).

Explanation: **God is your best friend. Do you want other friends? Then be a friend.**

FULFILLMENT

Definition: Completion; realization.

Meditation Verse: *"Open your mouth [life] wide and see if I [God] won't FILL it. You will receive every blessing you can use" (Psa. 81:10, TLB).*

Explanation: **God wants you to become a fulfilled person.**

FULL

Definition: Filled; complete; abundantly supplied.

Meditation Verse: *"Ask, and you will receive, that your joy may be FULL" (John 16:24, RSV).*

Explanation: **Open wide and receive.**

FUTURE

Definition: Time that is to come.

Meditation Verse: *"The good man ... has a wonderful FUTURE ahead of him. For him there is a happy ending" (Psa. 37:37, TLB).*

Explanation: **Tomorrow will be wonderful because God is wonderful.**

GENEROUS

Definition: Openhanded; ample; abundant.

Meditation Verse: *"It is possible to give away [be GENEROUS] and become richer! It is also possible to hold on too tightly and lose everything. Yes, the liberal man shall be rich! By watering others, he waters himself" (Prov. 11:24, 25, TLB).*

Explanation: **Generosity leads to generosity.**

GET

Definition: To obtain; acquire; receive.

Meditation Verse: *"If you give, you will GET! Your gift will return to you in full and overflowing measure, pressed down, shaken together to make room for more, and running over" (Luke 6:38, TLB).*

Explanation: **Getting should not be your first objective. But you will get when you follow God's plan.**

GIVE

Definition: To bestow without a return; to deliver.

Meditation Verse: *"GIVE your burdens to the Lord. He will carry them ..." (Psa. 55:22, TLB).*

Explanation: **Let God share your burdens.**

GLAD

Definition: To make happy; pleased; beautiful.

Meditation Verse: *"For thou, O Lord, hast made me GLAD by thy work; at the works of thy hands I sing for joy" (Psa. 92:4, RSV).*

Explanation: **With God working in you, there is rooted within you a sense of gladness that makes life worth living.**

GOAL

Definition: Objective; aim.

Meditation Verse: *"Have two GOALS: wisdom—that is, knowing and doing right—and common sense"* (Prov. 3:21, TLB).

Explanation: **Know and do right. It is not any harder, really, to aim at something thirty feet in the air than at something thirty feet away on the ground.**

GOOD

Definition: Pleasant; honorable; satisfactory.

Meditation Verse: *"Fix your thoughts on what is true and GOOD and right. Think about things that are pure and lovely, and dwell on the fine, GOOD things in others. Think about all you can praise God for and be glad about"* (Phil. 4:8, TLB).

Explanation: **Your total good is God's concern.**

GROW

Definition: To bring up, mature; thrive, flourish.

Meditation Verse: *"Happy are those who are strong in the Lord, who want above all else to follow your [God's] steps ... They will GROW constantly in strength ..."* (Psa. 84:5, 7, TLB).

Explanation: **God will lead you to grow every day as his child.**

GUIDANCE

Definition: Direction; leading.

Meditation Verse: *"Thou [God] dost GUIDE me with thy counsel ..."* (Psa. 73:24, RSV).

Explanation: **God promises to walk before you, a step at a time.**

HAPPINESS

Definition: Well-being; peace; comfort.

Meditation Verse: *"What HAPPINESS for those whose guilt has been forgiven!" (Psa. 32:1, TLB).*

Explanation: **Make no mistake about it—God has given you the inalienable, divine right to become a happy person!**

HARMONY

Definition: Lack of dissension; state of adaptation.

Meditation Verse: *"How wonderful it is, how pleasant, when brothers live in HARMONY!" (Psa. 133:1, TLB).*

Explanation: **God made you to be a "together" person … in harmony with yourself and others.**

HAVE

Definition: To hold in (one's) possession (with full title and right).

Meditation Verse: *"Because the Lord is my shepherd, I HAVE everything I need!" (Psa. 23:1, TLB).*

Explanation: **With the Lord in charge of your life, you are a "have" instead of a "have not."**

HEAL

Definition: To make well in body, mind, and soul.

Meditation Verse: *"Bless the Lord, O my soul, and forget not all his benefits, who forgives all your iniquity, who HEALS all your diseases" (Psa. 103:2, 3, RSV).*

Explanation: **God has the entire person in mind—body, mind, and soul. He is the great Physician.**

HELP

Definition: To aid, assist; to furnish with relief.

Meditation Verse: *"Fear not, for I [God] am with you. Do not be dismayed. I am your God. I will strengthen you; I will HELP you; I will uphold you with my victorious right hand"* (Isa. 41:10, TLB).

Explanation: **You have an unsinkable source of help—God.**

HOLD

Definition: To retain in love and affection; to have or keep.

Meditation Verse: *"The steps of good men are directed by the Lord ... If they fall it isn't fatal, for the Lord HOLDS them with his hand"* (Psa. 37:23, 24, TLB).

Explanation: **Because God has you in his hands, when you fall, you can rise. The fall is not fatal; staying down is!**

HOPE

Definition: Ground or source of happy expectation.

Meditation Verse: *"May the God of HOPE fill you with all joy and peace in believing, so that by the power of the Holy Spirit you may abound in HOPE"* (Rom. 15:13, RSV).

Explanation: **There is hope because there is God.**

HUMILITY

Definition: Submission; freedom from arrogance.

Meditation Verse: *"True HUMILITY and respect for the Lord lead a man [person] to riches, honor and long life"* (Prov. 22:4, TLB).

Explanation: **Humility is to think honestly of yourself, how big and wonderful God is, and who and what you can become under his guidance.**

INTELLIGENCE

Definition: Shrewdness; understanding.

Meditation
Verse:
"The INTELLIGENT man [person] is always open to new ideas. In fact, he looks for them" (Prov. 18:15, TLB).

Explanation: **God develops thinkers. He gives you the power of thought.**

JOY

Definition: State of happiness; the emotion excited by the expectation of good.

Meditation
Verse:
"These things I [Jesus] have spoken to you, that my JOY may be in you, and that your JOY may be full" (John 15:11, RSV).

Explanation: **Joy that affects the whole person—that is the joy God releases in you.**

KEEP

Definition: To carry on; to continue.

Meditation
Verse:
"[God] you love me! You are holding my right hand! You will KEEP on guiding me all my life with your wisdom and counsel; and afterwards receive me into the glories of heaven!" (Psa. 73:23, 24, TLB).

Explanation: **God is big enough to keep you in his care.**

KIND

Definition: Gentle; benevolent; having goodwill.

Meditation
Verse:
"And be KIND to one another, tenderhearted, forgiving one another, as God in Christ forgave you" (Eph. 4:32, RSV).

Explanation: **True kindness has never committed a harm.**

LIFE

Definition: The vital force; the state of being alive; that which excites or imparts spirit or vigor.

Meditation Verse: *"I [Jesus] am come that they might have LIFE, and that they might have it more abundantly" (John 10:10).*

Explanation: **Life is for living ... abundantly.**

LIGHT

Definition: Enlightenment; illumination.

Meditation Verse: *"You have turned on my LIGHT! The Lord my God has made my darkness turn to LIGHT!" (Psa. 18:28, TLB).*

Explanation: **God illumines you in love. The light of his love reveals more than darkness can possibly show up.**

LOVE

Definition: A feeling of strong personal attachment; goodwill.

Meditation Verse: *"We know how dearly God LOVES us, and we feel this warm LOVE everywhere within us because God has given us the Holy Spirit to fill our hearts with his LOVE" (Rom. 5:5, TLB).*

Explanation: **God loves you in spite of your shortcomings and failures.**

LOVE

Definition: To take delight or pleasure in.

Meditation Verse: *"For the Lord says, 'Because he LOVES me ... I will satisfy him with a full life and give him my salvation' " (Psa. 91:14, 16, TLB).*

Explanation: **God's love calls for the response of your love.**

MEDITATE

Definition: To contemplate; ponder.

Meditation Verse: *"Lord, here ... we MEDITATE upon your kindness and your love"* (Psa. 48:9, TLB).

Explanation: **God centers his thoughts on you so that you may center your thoughts on him.**

MOTIVATE

Definition: To impel; incite.

Meditation Verse: *"We can justify our every deed but God looks at our MOTIVES"* (Prov. 21:2, TLB).

Explanation: **We need to be motivated by God's Spirit; then we will be impelled to do good works.**

NEARNESS

Definition: Closeness.

Meditation Verse: *"I am always thinking of the Lord; and because he is so NEAR, I never need to stumble or to fall"* (Psa. 16:8, TLB).

Explanation: **God is near you to help you; he is closer than the air which you breathe.**

OPEN

Definition: Uncovered; free to be entered.

Meditation Verse: *"Ask and you will receive; seek and you will find; knock and the door will be opened to you. For everyone who asks will receive, and he who seeks will find, and the door will be OPENED to him who knocks"* (Matt. 7:7, 8, TEV).

Explanation: **God will answer.**

OPPORTUNITY

Definition: A fit time; a favorable set of circumstances.

Meditation Verse: *"So then, as we have OPPORTUNITY, let us do good to all men ..." (Gal. 6:10, RSV).*

Explanation: **You are given the chance every day to enrich the life of another person: a word, a deed, a prayer.**

PATIENCE

Definition: Forebearance; quality of being calm without discontent; undisturbed by obstacles, delays, failures.

Meditation Verse: *"We can rejoice, too, when we run into problems and trials for we know that they are good for us—they help us learn to be PATIENT" (Rom. 5:3, TLB).*

Explanation: **A problem can be turned into a power when you keep calm and keep working on the answer.**

PEACE

Definition: Freedom from fears, agitating passions, moral conflict; the end of hostilities.

Meditation Verse: *"So now, since we have been made right in God's sight by faith in his promises, we can have real PEACE with him because of what Jesus Christ our Lord has done for us" (Rom. 5:1, TLB).*

Explanation: **The warfare with your Maker is over. Peace with God paves the way for peace of mind.**

PEACE

Definition: A state of tranquillity or quiet.

Meditation Verse: *"And the PEACE of God, which passes all understanding, will keep your hearts and your minds in Christ Jesus" (Phil. 4:7, RSV).*

Explanation: **God brings tranquillity to your thoughts. In a sense, your peace of mind comes from a piece of his mind.**

PLAN

Definition: Project, program, outline, or schedule.

Meditation Verse: *"We can make our PLANS, but the final outcome is in God's hands. We should make PLANS—counting on God to direct us"* (Prov. 16:1, 9, TLB).

Explanation: **Always be planning something for tomorrow. Trust God for the results.**

PLEASURE

Definition: State of gratification; delight.

Meditation Verse: *"You have let me experience the joys of life and the exquisite PLEASURES of your own eternal presence"* (Psa. 16:11, TLB).

Explanation: **God has given you the joy and pure pleasure of being alive.**

PLENTY

Definition: Full supply; abundance.

Meditation Verse: *"But I keep right on praying to you, Lord.... You are ready with a PLENTIFUL supply of love and kindness ..."* (Psa. 69:13, TLB).

Explanation: **The way of God is meant to be the way of plenty for you.**

POWER

Definition: Energy; force; might.

Meditation Verse: *"To him [God] who is able to do so much more than we can ever ask for, or even think of, by means of the POWER working in us"* (Eph. 3:20, TEV).

Explanation: **The most fantastic power in the universe is now yours. Put it to good use.**

PRACTICE

Definition: To carry on; to exercise often or habitually.

Meditation Verse: *"Keep putting into PRACTICE all you learned ... and the God of peace will be with you"* (Phil. 4:9, TLB).

Explanation: **Practice is day-by-day application. Faith and works are excellent teammates.**

PRAISE

Definition: To acclaim; laud; express approval.

Meditation Verse: *"I will PRAISE the Lord no matter what happens ... Expect God to act! For I know that I shall again have plenty of reason to PRAISE him for all that he will do. He is my help! He is my God!"* (Psa. 34:1; 42:11, TLB).

Explanation: **You can praise God in every circumstance because you can advance even through adversity.**

PROTECT

Definition: To cover; shield; guard.

Meditation Verse: *"He [God] fills me with strength and PROTECTS me wherever I go"* (Psa. 18:32, TLB).

Explanation: **God surrounds you with his protective presence every moment.**

PURPOSE

Definition: The object aimed at; that which one sets before himself to be attained.

Meditation Verse: *"The Lord has made everything for his own PURPOSES ..."* (Prov. 16:4, TLB).

Explanation: **The ultimate purposes of your heavenly Father will prevail, and they are good.**

QUIETNESS

Definition: A state of rest; peace; relaxation.

Meditation Verse: *"And the effect of righteousness will be peace, and the result of righteousness, QUIETNESS and trust forever"* (Isa. 32:17, RSV).

Explanation: **Your right relationship with God is your assurance of inner quietness. Build on it.**

REFRESH

Definition: To revive; replenish; freshen up.

Meditation Verse: *"I [God] REFRESH the humble and give new courage to those with repentant hearts"* (Isa. 57:15, TLB).

Explanation: **Each day is the day for you to be replenished in your spirit.**

REJOICE

Definition: To feel and express joy or great delight.

Meditation Verse: *"This is the day the Lord has made. We will REJOICE and be glad in it"* (Psa. 118:24, TLB).

Explanation: **Celebrate! Let your happy spirit show!**

RELIEF

Definition: Comfort; ease; aid.

Meditation Verse: *"What RELIEF for those who have confessed their sins and God has cleared their record"* (Psa. 32:2, TLB).

Explanation: **God sees to it that you have a sense of relief inside. You are freed to become all you were meant to be.**

RENEW

Definition: To restore to freshness or vigor; to regenerate.

Meditation Verse: *"Your strength shall be RENEWED day by day like morning dew" (Psa. 110:3, TLB).*

Explanation: **Each day is an opportunity for you to renew the power required for successful living.**

RENEWAL

Definition: State or process of being made new again.

Meditation Verse: *"Put on the new self ... the new man which God, its creator, is constantly RENEWING in his own image, to bring you to a full knowledge of himself" (Col. 3:10, TEV).*

Explanation: **"Exciting renewal can be yours each day! Lovingly, your Friend, God."**

REST

Definition: Freedom from activity; cessation of motion.

Meditation Verse: *"It is senseless for you to work so hard from early morning until late at night, fearing you will starve to death; for God wants his loved ones to get their proper REST" (Psa. 127:2, TLB).*

Explanation: **You need to rest from routine and labor. God offers you rest of mind and body.**

RESTORE

Definition: To give back; to return; to reestablish.

Meditation Verse: *"Heal me, for my body is sick, and I am upset and disturbed. My mind is filled with apprehension and with gloom. Oh, RESTORE me soon" (Psa. 6:2, 3, TLB).*

Explanation: **The peace and joy you once enjoyed can be restored.**

REVERENCE

Definition: Honor or respect, felt or manifested, mingled with love and awe.

Meditation Verse: *"REVERENCE for God gives a man deep strength; ... REVERENCE for the Lord is a fountain of life ..." (Prov. 14:26, 27, TLB).*

Explanation: **You can respect your God. He respects you!**

RICH

Definition: Well-supplied; abundantly furnished.

Meditation Verse: *"You will give me added years of life, as RICH and full as those of many generations, all packed into one" (Psa. 61:6, TLB).*

Explanation: **God prospers you with a complete life.**

SAFETY

Definition: Freedom from danger.

Meditation Verse: *"We live within the shadow of the Almighty.... He alone is my refuge, my place of SAFETY; he is my God, and I am trusting him" (Psa. 91:1, 2, TLB).*

Explanation: **Everywhere you go, at all times, God has his arms around you.**

SALVATION

Definition: Deliverance; preservation from destruction.

Meditation Verse: *"The Lord is my light and my SALVATION; whom shall I fear?" (Psa. 27:1, TLB).*

Explanation: **The total salvation of God frees you from fear.**

SATISFACTION

Definition: State of being filled up; gratified.

Meditation Verse: *"You [God] open wide your hand to feed them and they are SATISFIED with all your bountiful provision"* (Psa. 104:28, TLB).

Explanation: **Are you satisfied? You can be!**

SELF-LOVE

Definition: Regard for one's own happiness.

Meditation Verse: *"You shall love the Lord your God with all your heart, and with all your soul, and with all your mind.... You shall LOVE your neighbor as YOURSELF"* (Matt. 22:37, 39, RSV).

Explanation: **People who hate others, hate themselves. Love for God grows a healthy love for yourself and those around you.**

SLEEP

Definition: Suspension of consciousness.

Meditation Verse: *"Then I lay down and SLEPT in peace and woke up safely, for the Lord was watching over me"* (Psa. 3:5, TLB).

Explanation: **God has his eye on you. Sleep deeply, peacefully, restfully.**

SMILE

Definition: A facial expression expressing pleasure, affection.

Meditation Verse: *"Trust in God! I shall again praise him for his wonderful help; he will make me SMILE again, for he is my God!"* (Psa. 43:5, TLB).

Explanation: **A smile spreads happiness. God wants your face to demonstrate his presence.**

SPIRIT

Definition: The agent of vital and conscious functions in man's being.

Meditation Verse: *"Create in me a clean heart, O God, and put a new and right SPIRIT within me"* (Psa. 51:10, RSV).

Explanation: **God guarantees you the spirit of newness and rightness so that you can become a growing person.**

STEADY

Definition: Constant; not fickle; unfaltering.

Meditation Verse: *"Keep traveling STEADILY along his pathway and in due season he will honor you with every blessing ..."* (Psa. 37:34, TLB).

Explanation: **Keep your hand on the plow and God will bring you to the happy outcome.**

STILL

Definition: Quiet; silence; calm.

Meditation Verse: *"Be STILL before the Lord, and wait patiently for him ..."* (Psa. 37:7, RSV).

Explanation: **Your mind and body are made to come to a halt at times. They need the rest.**

STRENGTH

Definition: The quality of being strong; capacity for endurance.

Meditation Verse: *That you will be filled with his [God's] mighty, glorious STRENGTH so that you can keep going no matter what happens–always full of the joy of the Lord"* (Col. 1:11, TLB).

Explanation: **Your strength depends on your resources. Is God your resource?**

SUCCESS

Definition: Attainment of a desired end.

Meditation Verse: *"Trust the Lord completely; ... In everything you do, put God first, and he will direct you and crown your efforts with SUCCESS"* (Prov. 3:5, 6, TLB).

Explanation: **Genuine success is the result of trust, God's guidance, and your efforts (your cooperation with God).**

SUCCESS

Definition: Favorable outcome of a venture.

Meditation Verse: *"Commit your work to the Lord, then it will SUCCEED"* (Prov. 16:3, TLB).

Explanation: **Don't be afraid of the word "success." Reminder: "God doesn't make any flops."**

SYMPATHY

Definition: Ability to enter into the feelings of another.

Meditation Verse: *"Be of one mind living like brothers with true love and SYMPATHY for each other, compassionate and humble"* (1 Pet. 3:8, Phillips).

Explanation: **God gives you feelings of sympathy with those who are close to you.**

THANKFULNESS

Definition: Kindly thought; acknowledgment of favor and kindness received.

Meditation Verse: *"Have no anxiety about anything, but in everything by prayer and supplication with THANKSGIVING let your requests be made known to God"* (Phil. 4:6, RSV).

Explanation: **Your love for God lifts your sights so that in everything you become thankful.**

OWNED

Definition: Possessed; kept.

Meditation Verse: *"I [God] have called you by name; YOU ARE MINE. When you go through deep waters and great trouble, I will be with you"* (Isa. 43:1, 2, TLB).

Explanation: **No more loneliness for you. You belong to God. He is with you in life.**

TRUST

Definition: Reliance on another's integrity.

Meditation Verse: *"TRUST in the Lord with all your heart,... In all your ways acknowledge him, and he will make straight your paths"* (Prov. 3:5, 6, RSV).

Explanation: **The God who has your total well-being in mind is the God you can totally trust in all of your ways.**

UNDERSTANDING

Definition: Discernment; comprehension; capability to reason.

Meditation Verse: *"I will run in the way of thy [God's] commandments when thou enlargest my UNDERSTANDING!"* (Psa. 119:32, RSV).

Explanation: **God wants you to better understand him, yourself, and others.**

VICTORY

Definition: Conquest, triumph; a successful outcome in a struggle.

Meditation Verse: *"Despite all this, overwhelming VICTORY is ours through Christ who loved us enough to die for us"* (Rom. 8:37, TLB).

Explanation: **Life may be overwhelming defeat or overcoming victory. You are born to triumph!**

VITALITY

Definition: Liveliness, vigor; power of enduring or continuing.

Meditation Verse: *"Trust and reverence the Lord,... then you will be given renewed health and VITALITY"* (Prov. 3:7, 8, TLB).

Explanation: **God will develop you into a lively person—whatever your age.**

WEALTH

Definition: An abundance of things desired; energies, faculties, and habits contributing to make people efficient.

Meditation Verse: *"The Lord's blessing is our greatest WEALTH ..."* (Prov. 10:22, TLB).

Explanation: **You are never poor when God is your Partner.**

WHOLENESS

Definition: Completeness; quality of being intact, total.

Meditation Verse: *"Jesus Christ maketh thee WHOLE: arise ..."* (Acts 9:34).

Explanation: **Through God, you become a total person.**

WILL

Definition: The choice or determination of one who has authority.

Meditation Verse: *"You can ask him [God] for anything, using my [Christ's] name, and I WILL do it, for this WILL bring praise to the Father because of what I, the Son, WILL do for you. Yes, ask anything, using my name, and I WILL do it!"* (John 14:13, 14, TLB).

Explanation: **God enjoys doing good things for you.**

WISDOM

Definition: Ability to reason soundly and deal with the facts; ability to discern what is true, proper, and right.

Meditation Verse: *"I will bless the Lord who counsels me; he gives me WISDOM in the night. He tells me what to do" (Psa. 16:7, TLB).*

Explanation: **Infinite intelligence is available to you.**

WORK

Definition: Exertion of strength or faculties to accomplish something.

Meditation Verse: *"Commit your WORK to the Lord, then it will succeed" (Prov. 16:3, TLB).*

Explanation: **Your work will be a success when you and it are consecrated to God.**

WORSHIP

Definition: To adore.

Meditation Verse: *"Let us WORSHIP and bow down, let us kneel before the Lord, our Maker! For he is our God ..." (Psa. 95:6, 7, RSV).*

Explanation: **God deserves our adoration because of who he is.**

WORTH

Definition: Of value; the quality of usefulness.

Meditation Verse: *"But God showed his great love for us by sending Christ to die for us while we were still sinners.... what blessings he must have for us now that we are his friends, and he is living within us!" (Rom. 5:8, 10, TLB).*

Explanation: **God's act of love through Christ has made us friends of God.**